BETWEEN
TWO
TRUTHS

BETWEEN TWO TRUTHS

LIVING WITH BIBLICAL TENSIONS

KLYNE SNODGRASS

Dean of Faculty and Paul W. Brandel
Professor of New Testament Studies
at North Park Theological Seminary

 Zondervan*Publishing*House
Grand Rapids, Michigan

A Division of HarperCollins*Publishers*

BETWEEN TWO TRUTHS: LIVING WITH BIBLICAL TENSIONS
Copyright © 1990 by Klyne Snodgrass

Requests for information should be addressed to:
Zondervan Publishing House
1415 Lake Drive, S.E.
Grand Rapids, Michigan 49506

Library of Congress Cataloging-in-Publication Data

Snodgrass, Klyne.
    Between two truths : living with biblical tensions / Klyne
Snodgrass.
        p. cm.
    Includes bibliographical references.
    ISBN 0-310-52891-7
    1. Christian life—Biblical teaching. I. Title.
BS680.C47S66   1990
248.4—dc20   90–33894
                                                                  CIP

Unless otherwise noted, all Scripture references are the author's own
paraphrase.

Edited by Michael G. Maudlin
Designed by Louise Bauer

Printed in the United States of America

90 91 92 93 94 95 / AK / 10 9 8 7 6 5 4 3 2 1

To my family—Phyllis, Nathan, and Valerie—
the people of the Evangelical Covenant Church
with whom I work
and friends from Crawford Avenue
all of whom have been patient with my tensions

Contents

Preface

I have often been asked to write on specific subjects to
satisfy the needs of other people. I wrote this book for
myself. For all my adult life I have struggled to
understand the Christian faith. I have always felt the
gospel called for more than most people give. In
addition, I have chafed when superficial answers are so
frequently offered for life's questions. At times part of
me has become annoyed enough to say, "Give me
Christ; you can have the Christians." The other parts of
me know that you cannot have Christ without his
people. The Bible will tolerate neither superficial answers
nor such separation.

The chapters in this book were originally independent addresses to lay people. I have brought them
together because they all deal with tensions in the
biblical message. After the first two chapters, which
provide a foundation for the others, the chapters can still
be read independently of each other. Therefore, this
book could serve conveniently as the basis for an adult
education series.

Dealing with tension has become the framework
within which I do much of my New Testament studies,
but this book is not intended for scholars. I have
eliminated footnotes and issues of scholarly concern
because this book is intended for laypeople who, like me,
struggle to live out their faith every day. Unless

otherwise specified, the translations of the biblical texts are my own renderings of the Greek and Hebrew scriptures.

I would like to thank my family and my colleagues at North Park Theological Seminary for their patience and assistance as I have worked on this manuscript. Appreciation is also expressed to Mickey Maudlin, who helped make the manuscript more readable, and to the people at Zondervan, who have assisted in bringing the work to completion.

To God be the glory.

Understanding Tension

1 Living with Tension

One of the most famous trials in history was that of Benjamin François Courvoisier in London in 1840, who is now immortalized in Madame Tussaud's Wax Museum. Courvoisier was a Swiss valet accused of slicing the throat of his elderly employer, Lord William Russell.

What made this trial notorious was the argument for the defense. The police had bungled the investigation. The evidence against Courvoisier was entirely circumstantial or had been planted. One of the officers had perjured himself, and the maid's testimony brought suspicion on herself. The defense attorney, Charles Phillips, was convinced of the innocence of Courvoisier and cross-examined witnesses aggressively.

At the beginning of the second day of the trial, however, Courvoisier confessed privately to his lawyer that he had committed the murder. When asked if he were going to plead guilty, he replied to Charles

Phillips, "No, sir, I expect you to defend me to the utmost."

Phillips was faced with a dilemma. Should he declare to the court that the man was guilty, or should he defend Courvoisier as best he could? Should he break the confidentiality of the client-lawyer relationship, or should he help a guilty man to possibly go free? Which is more important—truth or professional duty?

Phillips decided to defend the guilty man. But despite Phillips's efforts, Courvoisier was convicted. When the dilemma was later made public, Phillips's decision to defend a murderer horrified British society and brought him a great deal of criticism.

Living with Contradictions

Few of us face dilemmas as striking or as public as the one that faced Charles Phillips, but all of us have found ourselves caught on the horns of a dilemma. Life is like that, a balancing act between two competing ideals.

Often a simple act, such as casting a vote, involves us in tension. Should we vote for the candidate who takes the right moral stance but who is clearly less capable for the office? Sometimes such decisions are more personal, especially if the political game is as it is in Chicago. In a recent primary election our precinct captain came to my family, virtually begging for our votes. The polls showed that the party-backed candidate was clearly going to lose. If the candidate lost, the precinct captain would lose his job unless he could show that he had delivered the vote in his precinct and could transfer that loyalty to the new candidate. Should we vote for the candidate we prefer, or help a man to save his job? If we voted as he hoped, we might even get the trees we had requested a year earlier. (The notice that the trees would be planted arrived on election day!)

Randall works for a company that does business in a foreign country. Often he is expected to provide bribes to officials or employees of the companies with which he does business. Should he pay bribes in order to get the purchase contracts or should he refuse on ethical grounds? What if, instead of doing business, Randall worked for an agency providing food for the starving in Ethiopia? Should he pay the bribe in order to get the food to the poor?

My wife and I wrestled with the decision about where to send our children to school. Should we send them to the inferior, problem-plagued Chicago public school near our home, or should we send them to the better, private, Lutheran school nearby? If Christians do not work to make the public schools better, will the problems ever be solved? If our children do not get an adequate education, are we as parents being fair to them?

Experiencing tension is not limited to such issues. Dilemmas and hard choices permeate life. We only have to turn on the TV or open the newspaper to hear competing ideals pounded into us from our culture. Society tells us to be as tough as Rambo, but also as sensitive as Mr. Rogers. We, like Donald Trump, are to look out for "number one"; at the same time we are to be unselfish and caring, like Mother Teresa.

Many of our laws and court cases are attempts to find the balance between security and liberty. Both are basic human needs, but they exist in tension with each other. For instance, the freedom of the press and the interests of national security clash continually. Curfews, search warrants, drug testing, and surveillance are all practices that promote security but at the expense of liberty. Yet, unbridled liberty would make us victims of the whims of others, thus destroying our security.

We experience tension whenever we are faced with competing choices. The choice can be between two goods (such as choosing between flavors of ice cream), or between what we desire and what we know we should do (such as eating ice cream or sticking to our diet), or between two bad things (such as a mom's saying, "You can either eat your vegetables or skip dessert"). Whether the stakes are as weighty as God's moral laws or as common as watching your waistline, choices involve us in conflict, and conflict causes us to experience tension.

Tension is not confined to some alleged secular realm, nor is it merely a consequence of sinful living. It is also an inevitable aspect of a life of faith. In Ecclesiasticus, a book in the Apocrypha, we read: "Look at all the works of the Most High: they go in pairs, one the opposite of the other."

Tension permeates our faith. Every truth that we know is balanced by another truth that seems to be moving in the opposite direction. The gift of grace does not come without requirements. Freedom is not given without responsibility. In Christ we always have to deal with more than one reality at a time. Our faith is lived out between two or more competing truths, neither of which may be relinquished. We live between truths.

The focus on tension is not new. Christians have always wrestled with the fact that our faith gives us two or more realities that stand in tension or even in seeming contradiction with each other. "Double-truth" issues have dominated theological thinking throughout the church's history. We affirm both the humanity and the deity of Christ; the sovereignty of God and the free will of humanity; that humans are both sinful and yet created in the image of God. Throughout Christian history, heresy has resulted not from someone wanting to be evil or heretical but from someone taking a piece of the truth to an extreme and not doing justice to other truths as well.

Blaise Pascal wrote in his *Pensées* that "there are then a great number of truths, both of faith and morality, which seem contradictory, and which all hold together in a wonderful system" (861).

The origin of the focus on tension is the Bible itself. The unhappy "preacher" in Ecclesiastes 7:14–18 saw the complexity of life and warned against going to extremes. In 3:1–8 he points out that everything has its time, and the things that he lists are opposites (for instance, "a time to weep and a time to laugh"). The usual assumption in the Old Testament is that God blesses the righteous and punishes the guilty, but Job and the psalmists cry out that the innocent are oppressed and the wicked prosper (Job 12 and Psalm 73). The God who is so concerned to reveal himself to humanity is at the same time a God who hides himself (Isa. 45:15). Humans cannot see him and continue to live (Ex. 33:20). With one hand God prevents people from approaching because he is too holy; with the other hand he draws them to himself out of love.

Proverbs are designed to tell us what is generally true, but often proverbs conflict. Proverbs 26:4–5 places two "contradictory" proverbs back-to-back: "Do not answer a fool according to his folly, or you will be like him yourself. Answer a fool according to his folly, or he will be wise in his own eyes."

The New Testament, even more so than the Old Testament, is filled with examples of tension. Paul tells us, "For by grace you have been saved through faith. This is ... not from works, so that no one can boast" (Eph. 2:8–9). Yet, in James we read, "A person is justified from works and not from faith alone" (Jas. 2:24).

In Matthew 7:1 we are told not to judge, but in 7:16 we are told, "from their fruits you will know them." The "Prince of Peace" said in Matthew 11:29: "Take my yoke upon you and learn from me, because I am meek and lowly in heart, and you will find rest for your souls." But just before, in 10:34, he had said, "Do not think that I came to bring peace upon the earth; I did not come to bring peace, but a sword." The words of John 11:25–26 are intentionally contradictory: "The one believing in me, even if he should die, will live, and everyone living and believing in me will never die."

Paul was a master of writing about tension. Galatians 2:20 contains the startling words: "I am no longer living, but Christ lives in me. What I now live in the flesh, I live in the faith of the Son of God who loved me and gave himself for me."

In some ways tension is actually *increased* by belonging to Jesus Christ. It may seem strange to hear that biblical faith increases tension, but there is no question that it does. This tension is not destructive. Rather, it is peaceful and creative—but it is tension nonetheless.

There are perfectly good reasons why new tensions accompany the faith, for Christianity introduces new facts and forces into our lives that create tension. There are three new tensions that are *always* at work in Christian faith. They will be considered here, for they are foundational to the other tensions we will discuss. They are (1) the tension between gift and task, (2) the tension between the new age and the old, and (3) the tension of a life patterned on both the death and the resurrection of Christ.

Gift and Task

New life in Christ is both a *gift* and a *task*. The gospel both grants and demands life. Jesus granted limitless grace to his hearers when he invited tax collectors and sinners to the celebration of God's kingdom. But he also demanded limitless obedience from those who responded.

This tension can be summed up by the paradoxical command to "become what you already are in Christ."

We see this dynamic at work in many passages in scripture, where the writer goes from the *fact* of the gospel (what has been given) to the *commands* of the gospel (the task required). For instance, in Colossians, Paul states the *fact* that we have "died with Christ" (2:20 and 3:3) and then *commands* us to "put to death what belongs to your earthly nature" (3:5).

This blend between fact and command, gift and task, is quite common, particularly in the New Testament epistles. In 1 Peter 1:22–23 we read, "Since you have purified your souls in obedience to the truth so that you have unhypocritical brotherly love [*fact*], love each other fervently from the heart [*command*], because you have been born again [*supporting fact*]." In Romans 6:12 the command is given: "Do not let sin reign in your mortal body," while in Romans 6:14 the fact of the gospel is that "sin will not lord over you."

Such examples could be multiplied easily. The Christian life is lived out in the tension between gift and task in the pursuit of becoming what we already are in Christ.

This joining of gift and task is important, for it provides two necessary ingredients that prevent disaster in our lives. The dynamic between Christ's gifts and our tasks is the reason Christian tension is peaceful. The facts of the gospel allow us to relax and rest in God's grace, thus freeing us to deal creatively with the commands of the gospel.

The tension also prevents us from holding a do-nothing religion. We should not be misled to think that God's commands—such as, "Consider yourself dead to sin" (Rom. 6:11)—are pious examples of wishful thinking or an attempt at self-delusion. Rather, they are a call for us to make the gospel real in our lives. They ask us to take seriously what God has done in Christ and to view ourselves as God views us.

Jesus' parable of the unforgiving servant in Matthew 18:21–35 provides a sobering perspective on the nature of the tension between gift and task. Although the servant was forgiven an enormous debt, he harshly forced a fellow servant to pay a much smaller amount. His master judged him severely and asked, "Is it not *necessary* for you to show mercy to your fellow servant as I showed mercy to you?" We cannot claim the gift of God's forgiveness if we are not willing to do the task of forgiving others.

The New Age and the Old

A second major reason for tension in Christianity is the overlap between the new age and the old. (The Christian *new age* has nothing to do with the new age movement. The reality of newness in Christ is so central to

Christianity that we cannot give up this language.) In many ways this is the most important cause of tension in Christianity.

Jesus preached the kingdom of God. In the past, people often debated whether Jesus referred to some future kingdom (Matt. 19:28) or whether he meant that the kingdom had already come in his ministry (Matt. 12:28). There is widespread agreement now that *both* elements were part of Jesus' message. Justice can be done to Jesus' teaching only if we treat fairly both the kingdom as present and the kingdom as future.

The kingdom was *present* in that the promised end-time activity of God to defeat evil and establish righteousness was physically present in Jesus. In Luke 4:18–21 we witness Jesus reading Isaiah 61:1–2 in the synagogue. Afterward he declares, "Today this scripture is fulfilled in your hearing" (v. 21). The Judaism of Jesus' day associated this passage from Isaiah with God's end-time salvation. In effect, Jesus claimed that God's end-time salvation was here. The future kingdom had invaded the present. In the language of John 4:23, "the hour is coming and now is."

The same assumption of the new age in the midst of the old is expressed in the epistles. Well-known texts like 2 Corinthians 5:17 emphasize the present aspects of the kingdom: "If anyone is in Christ, that person is a new creation. Old things have passed away; behold new things have come into being." In Acts 2:16-21, prophecies concerning the last days are seen as fulfilled. Christians are those "upon whom the ends of the ages have come" (1 Cor. 10:11).

At the same time, there is an awareness that the ultimate victory of God will not occur until the second coming of Christ. Jesus proclaimed that the Son of Man will come in triumph (Matt. 24:30). At the Last Supper, he looked forward to the day he will banquet again with his followers in his father's kingdom (Matt. 26:29). If there is a belief that new things have come, there is also an awareness that God's triumph is not yet here. Life is lived in the midst of "a crooked and perverted generation" (Phil. 2:15). Second Timothy 1:10 can speak of death as abolished, but 1 Corinthians 15:26 indicates that death is the last enemy still to be abolished. We have been made alive in Christ and seated with him in the heavens (Eph. 2:5–6) so that our citizenship is in heaven (Phil. 3:20). But we also await future resurrection and know that our lives are still lived out on this earth. We live in the tension between the "now" and the "not yet."

An analogy that may help is that of a presidential transition team. Immediately after the election of a president in November, the victor appoints a transition team that initiates the transfer of power from one administration to the other. Although the victor is not president until inaugurated, the effect of that event is already at work in the transition. The outgoing president is virtually a lame duck, and the center of focus is on the incoming president and his new policies. The church is, in effect, a transition team.

Imagine being in a darkened room with heavy drapes over the windows. Suddenly someone opens the drapes so that you are able to see bright sunshine and a beautiful mountain view all around. You are still in the same room, but a new reality is perceived that changes what life is like in that room. Christians have experienced such a new reality in Christ so that life can no longer be as it was before.

The gospel can be summarized as the proclamation

of the new age in the midst of the old, since every theme of our faith is involved in this tension. Our salvation is both present and future. We have already been declared righteous (Rom. 5:1), but we wait for the hope of righteousness (Gal. 5:5). Eternal life is something that we already possess in the present, but we still await eternal life with God in the future. "We are *now* children of God, but it has *not yet* been made known what we will be" (1 John 3:2). The resurrection of Christ and the giving of the Spirit are the crucial factors indicating that the new age has dawned upon us. The presence of the Spirit makes real in our time the things that belong to God's end time. Our task as Christians is to make the new age real in the midst of the old.

If Christianity is founded upon the presence of the new age in the midst of the old and if all the themes of our faith partake of both present and future, the reasons for tension in our lives are clear. We are pulled by the forces of the old age, and at the same time we experience the effects of the new age. We do battle with ourselves: From which reality will we take our identity and "marching orders"?

A friend of mine is an executive in a major corporation. Recently he was told that he had to fire approximately five hundred employees. He knows the directive is unwise and motivated by greed and short-term profit. As a Christian he knows that he should act out of love and care for others, but the world, or the "old age," tells us to look out for ourselves and get ahead. Should he resign in protest and run the risk that someone uncaring will be given the task? Should he follow the directive and care for people as best he can? Whom should he decide to fire? Should he protect workers with families or make sure that he does not fire two people from the same family?

One area in which I feel the tension most strongly between the old age and the new is in attempting to help the poor. The reality of the new age requires that the love of God be extended to people in need. The reality of the old age is that it is sometimes dangerous and difficult to help needy people. I could get attacked and robbed by the very people I am trying to help. Even more likely, the help I give may make people dependent on me and provide no real escape from poverty. It would be very easy to turn my back on another person's need and say, "Let them work as I did." The presence of the new age will not allow such shirking of responsibility. I must help because I have been helped.

This dynamic tension between old and new was often misunderstood or taken to extremes in the early church. The church at Thessalonica was a church that focused so much on the future that some people neglected the present. They claimed that the Day of the Lord (an expression for the end-time coming of God) was already present. They thought it was no longer necessary to work (2 Thess. 3:10–11). The Corinthian church felt that they already possessed all there was to have. Some of them saw no need for a future resurrection (1 Cor. 15:12). From Paul's sarcastic words in 4:8–10 it appears that these people felt that they already had all that they needed and that they already reigned in God's kingdom. This overemphasis on what they possessed in the present led to their problems of pride and to their distortion of the gifts of the Spirit.

Similar errors still exist in our churches. Christians still fail to do justice to the fact that we live in two ages at the same time. For all practical purposes some have forgotten that there is a future triumph of God. They are content to focus only on this world. Others attempt to escape this world. They only focus on the future in heaven and are "on hold" in terms of doing anything beneficial with their faith. Healthy Christianity is a Christianity that knows both what it already has in Christ and what still awaits completion.

Death and Resurrection

The third reason for tension is the fact that Christian faith is an identification with both the death and the resurrection of Jesus Christ. The result is the curious injunction to gain life by dying to self.

Identification with the death and resurrection of Christ is virtually the same as Jesus' call to discipleship. We are called to deny self, take up our cross, and follow him (Mark 8:34). Giving up life in order to find it is the dynamic of the faith. There are many who are content to identify with the resurrection of Christ so that they experience joy and God's blessing, but they want nothing to do with identifying with his death in self-giving love. Christianity requires both.

Identification with the death and resurrection of Christ is a main theme in Paul's writings. The classic statement of this idea is found in Romans 6:4: "Therefore, we were buried with him through baptism into death in order that, just as Christ was raised from the dead through the glory of the Father, thus also we might live in newness of life." (See also 2 Cor. 4:10; Gal. 2:19–20; Col. 2:12–3:4.)

Through our oneness with Christ we are identified with Christ's death and resurrection. We should not view his death and resurrection merely as a way to take care of our sin. Christ's death and resurrection are mirrored in our day-to-day lives. The refusal to vent justifiable anger in order to show God's love is one way of mirroring Christ's death and resurrection. If because of God's work in me I give up my rights in order to accomplish God's purpose, I identify with Christ's death and resurrection. Any act in which we sacrifice our own will to make God's will possible is a means of dying and rising with Christ.

Death and resurrection are the pattern by which we live. Christians are to "know Christ and the power of his resurrection and the joint sharing in his sufferings as they are conformed to his death" (Phil. 3:10). Jesus' action of giving himself is to be lived by his followers, and the same Spirit that raised him is the Spirit by which we live.

It may seem incongruous to identify with death and resurrection at the same time, but according to the New Testament, we cannot identify with the resurrection without first and continually identifying with the death of Christ. The dynamic at work is a continual saying no to the possibility of a merely human existence, one that does not take God into account, and a continual saying "yes" to the way of the cross and the resurrection. That is what it means to say "Jesus is Lord."

Henri Nouwen, a writer and speaker on spirituality, experienced dying and rising when he left a successful teaching position at Harvard to become a member of a religious community caring for the mentally handicapped. There he discovered that he received more than he gave and that he had much to learn from those whom the world tends to view as inferior. Many of us know people who left lucrative careers to serve God, but we should not confine our thinking about dying and rising with Christ to such major moves of special people. All Christians are to live out Christ's dying and rising in much more common ways. We die and rise with Christ when, in keeping with God's intention, we choose to enhance a spouse, family member, or colleague rather than ourselves. Any time we give up what we are or what we want to be to become what God intends us to be, we have experienced dying and rising with Christ.

These three tensions—the call to become what we already are in Christ; to live according to the new age in the midst of the old age; and to find life through dying to self—are always at work in Christianity. That is why our faith is marked by a peaceful and creative tension.

In the next chapter we will see that not all tension is good tension, and we will find insight for handling tensions. In later chapters we will discover how the theme of "tension" helps us to understand ourselves, our faith, and our world.

Hopefully, as we deal with the tensions of living biblically, we will learn to say with Thomas Merton, "I have become convinced that the very contradictions in my life are in some ways signs of God's mercy to me." Tension is not merely a fact of life; in many ways tension is the joy of life. Through dealing adequately with tension we become the whole persons God intends us to be.

Understanding Tension

2 A Framework for Tension

At first I could hardly believe my ears. Barb was telling me that her experience as a short-term missionary in Zaire was much "easier" than her current life as a well-to-do suburbanite.

"In Zaire I had time to read and pray, was required to make few decisions, and ordered cheese from the city to share with my friends," she said. "Now I always have a million things to do, each entailing a dozen decisions. I barely find time to read, pray, or even be with friends."

She went on to describe how she feels torn between the "good life" and the call of Christ to a simple life. In the same day she interacts with the homeless and those housed in luxury. In the same mail she receives *Money Management* and *Sojourners* (a Christian magazine advocating radical discipleship with regard to the poor). No doubt Barb's life in Zaire was easy because she was only there for a short time. Life for career missionaries and

for all others who live in Zaire is tension-filled just like
life here in the United States.

Why can't life be simple? Why must there be so
many complications? Why do we have to live with
tension? These questions do not have easy answers, but
if we are to understand our tension-filled lives, we need a
framework for dealing with tension. This chapter seeks
to provide that framework by describing why we seek to
avoid tension, and the difference between good and bad
tension. It will explain how tension can be peaceful and
creative, and how accepting tension changes the way we
think of truth. Finally, this chapter will also identify the
virtues needed to cope with tension.

Forget the Simple Life

We do not like complexity and tension. In fact, in order
to keep life simple we will suppress those things that hint
at complexities. We accept partial truths, stereotypes,
and generalizations, even if they do not fit the facts:
"Poor people are always lazy; if only they would work."
"I don't have to worry about the hungry or the homeless
because they don't live near me. They're someone else's
problem." Even the Bible is kept simple. We read our
favorite passages and conveniently ignore others that call
our lifestyles and theology into question. "Surely," we
say, "Jesus did not intend that we should really share our
possessions." Our attempt to make life and faith simple
derives from our need to find some handle by which to
control the complexity around us.

Nevertheless, we cannot escape the complexity of
life. It is in us—in our minds, our bodies, our
personalities, and our relationships. We need both to be
alone and to be with people. We need independence,

and we need approval and a sense of belonging. We enjoy both being lazy and the satisfaction of having worked hard. The failure to deal with the tensions only creates problems. As Gail Sheehy points out in her book *Passages*, issues pushed down in one period of life tend to swing up in the next one with added wallop. Every loose end not dealt with will resurface to haunt us.

If it is true that human life is complex, then we ought to stop acting as if it were not. Enjoying the "simple" life is one thing, but being simplistic by ignoring or rationalizing away the complexity of life will not work. Elton Trueblood's words are fitting:

> One of the best contributions which Christian thought can make to the thought of the world is the repetition that life is complex. It is part of the Christian understanding of reality that all simplistic answers to basic questions are bound to be false. Over and over, the answer is *both-and* rather than *either-or*.

The immediate objection comes to mind that some of the finest Christians we know are people with a simple faith who live uncomplicated lives. Surely Mother Teresa doesn't have to deal with tension. If "simple faith" means undivided loyalty to Jesus Christ, then I, too, would emphasize that this is the source of peace. But I would not agree that such a commitment removes the problems human beings face. Mother Teresa—like the rest of us—faces tension all the time. Should she use her time actually helping the sick and dying in India or should she spend her time traveling to raise money? Which sick and dying should she help? Should she use her limited resources only on patients sure to recover, and ignore the dying? When we think life is simple, we only show we are unaware of the problems.

The rosy picture presented by some evangelists and religious broadcasters that a strong faith guarantees a problem-free life is a perversion of the gospel. Their views suggest that Christians always recover from illness and always enjoy financial blessing. People like to hear such messages, but misunderstanding and heartache are the frequent results. The Jesus who chose the way of the cross would feel ill at ease summarizing his message as "something good is going to happen to you." The gospel does not guarantee a trouble-free life, nor does it promise to make us rich. Such claims do not fit the Bible.

The statement that we should love our neighbor as ourselves is a simple statement. But often it is not so simple to know what the loving thing to do really is. What should a teacher do with a student who has been caught cheating? What should a teacher tell a student who does not have the potential for his or her chosen career?

My concern is not to make the Christian life appear difficult, but to ensure that we deal honestly with all aspects of the life that God has given us. Life is complicated. There is no way to get around that fact.

Getting Rid of Bad Tension

Not all the tension we experience as Christians, however, is "good" tension. More frequently we experience negative tension that comes from anxiety and lack of direction. If there is tension in our lives because we do not trust God or if we are unsure whether we will obey him, that tension is destructive.

Another serious negative tension is the conflict between good and evil within us. In Romans 7:13–25 the apostle Paul describes how the right thing that he wants to do is not what he does; instead, the wrong thing that he does not want to do is the very thing that he does. We are all familiar with his plight. We know that we should follow Christ and serve God, but there is also in us the desire to choose our own way and serve ourselves. We know that life is not measured by possessions, but advertising and credit cards seduce us into trying to buy happiness. The way of Christ beckons us, but the self-serving philosophy of this world calls just as loudly.

Yet another form of negative tension is the *refusal to be human*. Destructive tension is caused by our attempts to deny the limitations of our humanity. To be human is to have to deal with tensions and incompleteness. The failure to do so only makes matters worse. We are fragile and finite, temporary, and dependent on each other and especially on God, but we do not like to admit it. The problem is as old as the story of the Garden of Eden. The temptation was to eat the fruit and be like God, knowing both good and evil. In effect, the temptation was to escape incompleteness. The most common form of this temptation, especially when we are young, is the denial of the reality of death.

The refusal to be human is the ultimate definition of sin. Most of us prefer to ignore our limitations and act as if we are the measure of reality. We want to be like God. We want to be independent, to choose our own way, and to be our own person. We do not want to admit the truth about ourselves, especially with regard to our sin. We do not want to live the lives that God has given us. How frequently have we seen a person present a model of godliness and propriety, only to find out later that it was all a sham, that the person was filled with pride and insensitivity, and in the end was a failure. Such tragedies have their origin in the refusal of people to be human.

Experiencing these negative forms of tension often leaves us feeling that we are standing in quicksand. The good news is that God has provided a foundation for life in Jesus Christ. To affirm that he is Lord is to cut through our anxiety and lack of direction and to be put in touch with reality itself. We can never understand "good tension" if the real issue in our lives is the "bad" tension of not deciding whether to follow Christ or "go it on our own."

Peaceful and Creative Tension

Following Christ, however, is no simple matter. The negative tension is removed, but new tension is introduced. As C. F. D. Moule put it, the Christian faith is characterized by a "peaceful and creative tension." The words, at first glance, do not seem to go together, but they accurately describe the New Testament message.

Tension in the Christian life is not like a tightrope where we must fear falling off either side. There would be no peace in that. A more appropriate image is that of a stringed instrument. Properly attached at the two right places, the instrument can be played. If a string is left loose, music cannot be produced. If it is stretched too tightly, the string will break.

Neither does such talk of tension in Christian living refer to anxiety, tenseness, or being destroyed by conflicting options. Nor is there reference to uncertainty, relativity, or straddling the fence. To speak of complexity does not imply that the gospel is confusing.

The gospel is clear and is often reducible to simple, basic ideas such as "Abba" (Jesus' unique address to God as Father), "covenant," "love," or "the death and resurrection of Christ." But if each of these expressions represents a simple statement of the gospel, none of them is simplistic. On the contrary, they all are doorways into a new reality that encompasses all of life.

As we will find as we look at various issues from the New Testament, the message of tension within the Christian faith is essentially a discussion of the grace of God. That is why the tension within the Christian faith is first of all peaceful. It is based on the grace of God that has been revealed in Christ. Here is the foundation for life.

Grace is never just pure gift, however; it is also a call to responsibility, and this is why the tension is creative.

Our peace has its own struggles. If grace tells us, "You are God's child," it also instructs us, "Now live like it." We have for too long viewed faith as something we "got" at some point, but our relationship with God is a *process* of living with him. Therefore, the tensions we experience become the stage on which our faith is given creative expression. Working through our struggles and the complexities of life allows us to grow as individuals.

I have a friend whose wife left him and his sons. He did not doubt God's love, but he questioned how God could allow this and ached over why his prayers were not answered. He found no quick fixes for the hurts of life. But through wrestling with his concerns, his faith has grown and he has pieced his life together to become a useful person for God's purposes. He has dealt with the tensions and found grace.

The call to life in Christ is a call to real life. The

possibilities within that call are as varied as are the persons who respond to it. A God who will not create two snowflakes alike surely does not mean to stifle human creativity and possibility.

Nor is life with Christ a simplistic existence. Those who think that they can encompass or master life in Christ are in for a surprise. As one person put it, Jesus is an inspiring and disturbing presence. He inspires us and comforts us, but he also takes us apart and disturbs us. God accepts us as we are, which is a source of great comfort. But soon, if we are at all attentive, his presence becomes a convicting and transforming power forcing change, sometimes even painful change. As that change is effected, we know once again the comfort of grace, but the process is not over. Again and again God comforts and disturbs, and comforts and disturbs.

Life in Christ is not an easy life, for we are called to grow continually by following in the way of the cross. Christians always live on the edge. We remain open to God's future and give ourselves to the tasks to which he calls us.

Accepting tension allows us to relax and accept life as it is. One evening after I finished speaking about tension, a woman said, "Thank you. I was beginning to think I was crazy." Acknowledging tension gives relief from the fear that "Something must be wrong, for everything seems in conflict." Accepting tension will not remove the competing forces, but it does allow us to tell the truth about our lives.

Christian maturity, then, requires that we live honestly with biblical tensions. As one British theologian put it, "Anyone unfortunate enough not to experience tensions . . . is a very superficial person indeed, a non-starter in the Christian stakes."

The Whole Truth

Once the Devil was walking along with one of his cohorts. They saw a man ahead of them pick up something shiny. "What did he find?" asked the cohort. "A piece of the truth," the Devil replied. "Doesn't it bother you that he found a piece of the truth?" asked the cohort. "No," said the Devil, "I will see to it that he makes a religion out of it."

Understanding and accepting tension changes how we view truth. Too often Christians are content to possess a piece of the truth. If not a religion, at least they make a denomination from the partial knowledge. The root problem is usually a very narrow understanding of the nature of truth.

By *truth* we usually mean "true statements or facts," somewhat akin to Detective Joe Friday's "Just the facts, Ma'am." Many times the Bible does use "truth" with reference to true facts. The Bible's concept of truth, however, is much broader than this.

The Old Testament word usually translated "truth" is from the root that means "firm" or "stable." Often the word carries the connotation of "faithfulness, trustworthiness, or steadiness." The principal idea is that truth can be relied on. When truth is used of people or God, the emphasis on reliability assumes that truth is *relational*. Truth in this case is correspondence between words and actions. Truth assumes a relationship where expectations are fulfilled, claims are met, and confidence is justified.

When John in his gospel describes the *logos* (the Word) as full of grace and truth (1:14), the point is not that Jesus is full of grace and facts. Rather, in him we see a new revelation of the reliable God Moses knew. God has brought a new truth into being in order to accomplish salvation and show his faithfulness. Jesus embodied this new reality to such an extent that he could be called "the truth."

Truth, then, in the Bible is a multifaceted concept. This is important. If truth is understood merely as not telling a lie, it becomes easy for us to equate truth with the reality that we ourselves see. We think we can grasp the truth; we remain oblivious to the fact that much of reality—much of God's truth—has not even been considered by us.

But no human can perceive God's reality as it really is any more than he or she can concentrate on every facet of a diamond at the same time. In Jesus Christ we find all truth, but only he encompasses the truth.

Repeatedly the scripture makes the point that God's ways are far beyond human perception. First Corinthians 13:12 expresses this in a way that should inject humility into all of us: "For now we see dimly through a mirror . . . now we know in part." We have been bound to the one who is truth himself, but we only know in part. Truth is much larger than humans can encompass. If our knowledge is always partial at best, then we should not be surprised to experience tension in the Christian life, or to find it in places we did not expect.

If truth is broader than humans collectively can grasp, truth is certainly broader than we as individuals can grasp. No one person can perceive all the truth that is available to humanity. The point is not merely that there are fields of expertise. Rather, no individual can experience enough or learn enough to do justice to the complexity of our lives. We need each other to understand truth. That is part of what it means to be human.

The Prime Virtues

So far, we have affirmed that life is complex, that truth is larger than we had thought, and that our faith in Christ is structured around new tensions. But given all these complicating aspects to life, how then are we to live?

Scripture provides three "prime virtues" that are to guide us as we make our way down life's various paths: they are *love, wisdom,* and *integrity.*

Love is the foundation of all our relationships and the expression of our faith. Love is the absolute essential ingredient in all we do. Regardless of how many tensions we recognize, if love does not direct our actions, we are wrong. Nor should we assume that love and truth will be in tension with each other or that love will seek to evade the truth. First Corinthians 13:6 states that love *rejoices* with the truth. If God is characterized by love, certainly his people must be as well. But love does not exist as the sole virtue to guide us. Even love must be instructed by wisdom and integrity. Otherwise our love may degenerate into selfish bias and injustice.

Wisdom is needed to guide us as we make decisions about the competing forces causing our tensions. Wisdom is a dominant theme in both testaments. Certain Old Testament books are classified as "wisdom literature" because they focus on wisdom for right living. (These books include works like Job, Proverbs, and Ecclesiastes and also Apocryphal books like the Wisdom of Solomon and Ecclesiasticus.) Many other Old Testament books also focus on wisdom as well so that the message is clear: To live correctly before God is to practice wisdom.

The New Testament emphasizes wisdom just as strongly. Like most letters in the ancient world, nearly all of Paul's epistles contain a prayer just after the initial words of greeting. Often Paul's prayer is a request for wisdom and understanding so that the people will know how to live their lives in Christ. The prayer for the Philippians is particularly instructive: "I pray that your love may increase yet more and more in knowledge and understanding so that you may approve the things that really matter" (Phil. 1:9–10; see also Eph. 1:17–19; 3:14–19; Col. 1:9–12). In effect, Paul prays that they will have wise love.

When the Bible focuses on wisdom, usually the concern is for moral discernment, discretion, and practical skill. The real issue is the ability to read a situation and make the appropriate decisions for right living. Should fetal tissue be used to treat disease? Should a mother agree to give money to an adult son who is married and has one child, but neither he nor his wife is employed? If she does, will she only deplete her resources and increase his dependency? If she does not, will she cause estrangement and unnecessary hardship?

We should not think that the call to wisdom is merely to an intellectual or academic approach to life. In James 3:13 we read: "Who is wise and understanding among you? Let that person demonstrate his works from good conduct done in the humility that comes from wisdom." The call to wisdom is a call to productive and practical discernment.

The third prime virtue is *integrity*. Integrity is needed to make sure that we act responsibly with the tension that confronts us. It will not allow us to slight any of the truths or persons that we face. The word *integrity* does not appear often in translations of the Bible, but one of the main purposes of scripture is to bring integrity to our lives. The repeated commands in the Bible to speak truth are really a call to integrity. If a person has integrity, he or she is a "unified whole." There is unity between what is said and what is done. An employer may claim to care about his or her employees, but if the treatment of the employees is determined only by the profit margin, that employer does not have integrity. Honesty is required not only in our relations with each other, but even more important—we must be honest with ourselves and with God.

Once a student lost an argument defending what he thought was right. Upon smugly telling his grandmother of his experience and expecting to be commended by her, he was shocked when she retorted, "If history is to remember you at all, it will be for the quality and integrity of your compromises." The word "compromise" ought not cause alarm. We all make numerous compromises each day as we wrestle with our tensions. The grandmother was right. What counts is the *quality* and *integrity* of our compromises between the truths facing us.

In his book *Loving God,* Charles Colson draws attention to an incident involving an Indiana judge named William Bontrager. Bontrager had to pass sentence on Fred Palmer, a decorated Vietnam veteran who was found guilty of burglary. The crime was caused partly by involvement with drugs and alcohol. Indiana law required a sentence of ten to twenty years for Palmer's offense. However, new regulations designating a lesser penalty had gone into effect eighteen days *after* Palmer's arrest. To complicate matters, Palmer had become a Christian in jail and seemed to have changed. Should the judge sentence Palmer, a man who had never been in jail, to ten years or more? Or should he declare the older statute in violation of Indiana's constitution and give him a lighter sentence? Bontrager did the latter. Fred Palmer was out of jail in seven months, had a job, and was paying back his former victims.

The events that followed received national attention. The Indiana Supreme Court reversed the judge's decision and ordered Fred Palmer sent back to prison. The judge's attempts to fight the court's decision during the next two years led to his own indictment for criminal contempt of court and, finally, his forced resignation. Fred Palmer was sent back to prison, only to be released twenty months later by the governor. Bontrager's convictions cost him his job, but not his integrity.

Most of us are not judges and do not find ourselves in such public dilemmas. We all frequently face circumstances, however, where ethical decisions pull us in different directions. Too often we merely choose the course of least resistance. The real issue is the quality and integrity of our decisions. What do we do when there are tensions between legitimate, conflicting demands? If our decisions justly deserve to be called loving and wise—and show integrity, then we have done what we should have.

May God keep us from the fanaticism of the extremes and the mediocrity of the middle of the road!

Understanding Ourselves

3 Saint and Sinner

Country music is not usually my cup of tea, but when Waylon Jennings described himself in "The Gemini Song," he was describing all of us:

> When I'm bad, I'm bad
> And when I'm good, I'm the best you ever
> seen. . . .
> There's two sides to me, and we ain't even
> friends.

In Christ we are a new creation, but that does not mean the old has gone away. There are still "two sides" to us that "ain't even friends." We still struggle with right and wrong. A friend once confessed to me: "At the very moment that I am singing a hymn of praise, I am thinking inappropriate thoughts about a woman a few pews ahead. When I am helping other people, I think about how 'good' I am appearing to them." We all are guilty of such contradictions.

We desire both the right and the wrong. As the Roman philosopher Seneca put it, "People love their vices and hate them at the same time; they hate their sins and cannot leave them."

The same David who wrote psalms and danced before the Lord also committed adultery and murder. The same Peter who witnessed Jesus' miracles and was the first to confess Jesus as the Messiah went on to deny him three times. If we take a searching look at ourselves, we know that we, too, are capable of both good and evil.

We have been created in the image of God, with a moral awareness and a need to be in relation to God and follow his ways. On the other hand, we also possess the desire to choose our own way, to be independent of God. Paul describes the dilemma this way: "I don't know what I am doing! I am not doing what I want; rather, I am doing the very thing I hate" (Rom. 7:15). He is describing what we all experience.

In the words made famous by Martin Luther, we are *simul iustus et peccator,* at the same time *saint* and *sinner.* Neither of those words makes us comfortable, but both are true of Christians. Paul described our situation by saying, "The flesh has desires contrary to the Spirit and the Spirit has desires contrary to the flesh" (Gal. 5:17). As one person put it: "The old man has been drowned in baptism, but the rascal can swim!" There is a new reality for those in Christ to make right living possible. On the other hand, there is an old tendency toward sin, which has not been destroyed. God has not seen fit to make us into righteous robots.

The way Luther worded this expression is important. We are not *part* sinner and *part* saint, nor are we sometimes one and then the other. We are *at the same time* saint and sinner. Even when we are performing the most sacred act, we do so as sinners. And when we are guilty of sin, we are still saints. This tension of being at the same time saint and sinner merely makes personal the tension we saw before, between living simultaneously in the old age and the new. Both are *in* us.

On Being a Saint

Who wants to be a saint? In our day the term suggests something austere and unnatural, a freak, or at least someone with an almost visible halo. Only a deluded person would consider himself or herself a saint. It does not help to learn that the word usually translated as "saints" in the King James Version literally means "holy ones." "Holy" is not any better than "saint." We don't qualify for either.

To think of being a saint as something akin to earning a merit badge is to misconstrue badly how the Bible uses the term.

When the New Testament describes people as "saints" or "holy ones," the thought is *not* first of all about moral behavior. It is about position.

The word *holy* describes something separated or set apart. God is holy because he is separated from humans. He cannot be grouped with them as the same kind of being. Paul refers to the Corinthians as "sanctified in Christ Jesus, called to be saints" (1 Cor. 1:2). People who are *sanctified* are those who have been set apart by God, even if they are not living holy lives as they should (which was definitely true of the Corinthian church). The point in all three terms—*sanctified, called,* and *saints*—is to emphasize that God has separated us to himself and has given us a new standing in Christ.

To be a saint only means to be separated to God. It

refers to God's action, not ours. This does not relieve us of the responsibility for holy living, but we cannot live separated lives until we have been separated. Because God has separated us to himself, we are to live in conformity with who he is. He has commanded us, "Be holy, because I am holy" (1 Peter 1:16). Of course, God has also given us the gift of the Holy Spirit to make holy living a possibility.

On Being a Sinner

Just as Christians are confused about what it means to be a saint, so, too, there is much confusion over what it means to be a sinner.

If we ask ourselves, "Did I sin today?" most of us would think in terms of whether we had broken some commandment. Unless we had done something obviously wrong, we might think, "No, I did not commit any sin I can think of." That would be a very narrow view of sin and would prevent us from seeing how large the problem of sin really is for all of us. To see sin as the "bad" things we do enables some Christians to delude themselves into believing in perfectionism, the belief that we may reach a point in this life when we no longer sin.

Sin is much more than acts that we commit. A biblical view of sin is multifaceted. The Old and New Testaments use a variety of words and ideas to explain the concept: missing the mark, falling, disobedience, rebellion, guilt, and uncleanness. The Bible also describes unintentional sins, deliberate sins, and sins of omission.

In the previous chapter I explained that the ultimate definition of sin is the refusal to be human. Generally, we can say sin is any failure to be the persons God created us to be. God created us to live in meaningful relation with him and each other. That includes being involved in his purposes, having his attitudes, and being in tune with his desires. In effect, sin is a bad trade. Sin is the rejection of God's intention for us in favor of something of far less value. (See Rom. 1:21–23.)

A few years ago Roy Whetstine went to a rock exhibition to buy an agate for each of his sons. At one table he saw some stones in a Tupperware container marked "Any stone fifteen dollars." He picked up a potato-sized rock and asked, "You want fifteen dollars for this?" The man said, "I'll give it to you for ten dollars, since it is not as pretty as the agates." Roy bought the stone and could hardly contain himself. He had just purchased the largest known star sapphire— 1,509 carats—valued at $2.5 million uncut and about ten million cut. That is the kind of bad trade sin is. Sin is the sacrifice of priceless sapphires for pretty agates.

To be more specific, sin should be described as a sphere within which we live. Humans have traded relation with God for a sphere whose structure does not make room for God. The New Testament writers refer to this "structure" with such phrases as "this present evil age" or "the course of this world." It is this kind of life that is in mind when Paul says, "Do not be conformed to this age" (Rom. 12:2), or when John says, "Do not love the world nor the things in the world" (1 John 2:15). Even where there is no disobedience of some specific law, living according to the "world" is living in sin. I may not have broken any commandment, but if I define "success" and "necessities" according to a structure that has no room for God, I am sinning.

Closely related is the identification of sin as *the*

rejection or ignoring of God in order to live on our own. It is allowing ourselves to be determined only by ourselves. Martin Luther hit the nail on the head when he defined sin as a human being curved in upon himself or herself. In failing to acknowledge God, people become diverted from God and inverted upon themselves. We become like shavings planed from a piece of wood that naturally curl around themselves. We become separated from the source of life. Our thinking, our perceptions, our ways of knowing all become distorted.

Paul describes all this as "living according to the flesh." By "flesh" he means that which is "merely human." Sin is the attempt to find life and happiness only within the reach of human possibilities.

This is not to suggest that human possibilities are bad. On the contrary, they are good *in relation to God.* We can easily recognize blatant forms of sin such as committing crimes, taking drugs, lying, committing adultery, quarreling, and so on. But often sin does not look bad. Sin is good possibilities used for wrong purposes and without reference to God. Not surprisingly then, sin can be something that initially looks good to us. We gleefully draw it into our lives only to be taken captive by it. Suddenly we become oriented to ourselves rather than to God, and then we are caught in the trap. For example, earning money is a good enterprise, but it is easy for us to be trapped by money so that we become obsessed by it. Money then controls us and traps us in sin. Desires, experiences, or relationships that start out as good and wholesome can turn into traps that cause our downfall. All too familiar are such incomprehensible acts as pastors running off with church secretaries. This is what happens to people inverted around themselves, who use good things for the wrong purpose. Christians should not think they are immune from such traps.

One other description of sin is necessary. Sin is a power or tyrant—a force field—that tries to dominate us. In fact, Paul usually refers to "sin" in the singular rather than to "sins." One of the most important statements of the early church was "Jesus is Lord," which is about salvation as much as it is about Christ. Salvation involves a change of lordships; we are transferred from a place where sin is lord to one where Jesus is Lord. Sin is personified and viewed as a tyrant who manipulates people. It is like an addictive drug that takes control. By focusing on their own desires, people actually become slaves of sin.

To summarize, sin is a way of life that ignores God and focuses on itself. It is a manipulative power, and it also includes specific acts of disobedience. Only a view of sin that encompasses all these factors is broad enough to help us combat the reality of our sin.

Sinless Sinners

The Epistle of 1 John helps us to understand this tension between being both saint and sinner in the Christian life. This simple but profound letter has caused a great deal of difficulty for commentators because two sections of the book seemingly contradict each other. In 1:6–2:2 we read:

> If we claim to have fellowship with him yet are living in darkness, we are lying and are not doing the truth. But if we are living in the light, as he is in the light, we have fellowship

with one another, and the blood of Jesus, his Son, is cleansing us from all sin.

If we claim that we do not have sin, we are deceiving ourselves and the truth is not in us. If we confess our sins, he is faithful and just so that he forgives our sins and cleanses us from all unrighteousness. If we claim that we have not sinned, we make him a liar and his word is not in us.

My dear children, I write this to you so that you will not sin. But if anybody does sin, we have one who speaks to the Father in our defense—Jesus Christ, the Righteous One. He is the atoning sacrifice for our sins, and not for ours only, but also for the sins of the whole world.

The author rejects several statements of his opponents and offers instruction about sin. He makes the following points: (1) Claiming to have fellowship with God while still living a sinful life ("living in darkness") is a lie. (2) Living properly ("living in the light") brings fellowship with each other and cleansing through Christ's sacrificial death. (3) If people claim that sin is not in them or that they have not committed sin, they are lying to themselves and are out of touch with the truth. (4) Confession of sin leads to forgiveness and cleansing. (5) Christians should not sin, but when they do, Jesus Christ intercedes for them and is the means of the restoration of their relationship with God.

Clearly, the author was objecting to claims of some to be without sin or guilt. He rejects perfectionism as a possibility and presents a theology of ongoing confession, forgiveness, and cleansing through Christ.

But then we come to 3:4–10:

Everyone doing sin is also doing lawlessness;
in fact, sin is lawlessness. You know that he
appeared so that he might take away our sins,
and there is no sin in him. No one remaining
in him keeps on sinning. Everyone who keeps
on sinning has neither seen him nor known
him.

Dear children, let no one deceive you. The
person doing righteousness is righteous just as
Christ is righteous. The person doing sin is of
the devil, because the devil has been sinning
from the beginning. For this reason the Son of
God appeared–that he might destroy the
devil's works. Everyone who has been born of
God is not doing sin, because God's seed
remains in him. He is not able to go on
sinning, because he has been born from God.
This is how the children of God and the
children of the devil are made known: everyone
who is not doing righteousness is not from
God; nor is anyone who is not loving his
brother.

This passage seems to be a direct contradiction of
1:6–2:2. Earlier John had said that if we say that we do
not sin, we are liars. Here we find that the one remaining
in Christ is not sinning and is not able to be sinning
because God's "seed" remains in him or her. Furthermore, the one sinning does not know Christ, but is from
the Devil. Have both passages come from the same
hand?

Although there is still considerable debate about

these texts, both make statements that are true and necessary.

The problem John was addressing contained two errors. Some people claimed to be living in such close fellowship with God that they no longer sinned. A heretical perfectionism was the result. Second, despite claims of fellowship with God, these people were living as if God made no difference in their lives. The teaching in 1:6–2:2 was designed to help the readers understand the presence of sin in all humans and the means of forgiveness and cleansing in Christ. That alone, however, would not solve the problem, for people would still be living lives antithetical to Christ.

Much of the rest of the letter describes the life required of Christians. The purpose of the letter is summed up in 2:6: "The one claiming to remain in Jesus ought to live as he lived." A Christian cannot go on sinning as if being in Christ made no difference. If there has been no change so that love dominates life, then there has been no rebirth (see 2:9–11; 3:17; 4:20–21). It is this aspect of the teaching that is in view in 3:4–10. While a sinless perfectionism is to be rejected, our rebirth excludes a sinful way of life.

A helpful way to understand 3:4–10 is to focus on the tenses of the Greek verbs. When the writer speaks of sinning, he puts it in the present tense. This would stress that the action is continual. Note 3:6, "No one remaining in him *keeps on sinning*," and 3:9, "... *is not able to be sinning*." The focus is on a life *characterized* by sin. Those in Christ cannot live a sinful lifestyle, for rebirth has placed God's "seed" (either the Spirit or the Word) in them. Those who live a life characterized by sin do not have God as their Father.

The truth of both 1:6–2:2 and 3:4–10 is evident.

We cannot escape the reality of sin in our lives. The denial of sin and its guilt is delusion and evidence of distance from God. Sin is to be confessed, and forgiveness and cleansing are to be found in Christ. On the other hand, sin is not to be taken for granted nor is it to be practiced. Those in Christ cannot live a life characterized by sin.

The church today needs to hear this message. The work of God that accomplished our conversion is to be continually at work in us, changing our lives and motivating us to share God's love. We are sinners continually, but we are also saints continually because God has accomplished something new in us.

Life as Saint-Sinners

Although being simultaneously a saint and a sinner creates tension in the Christian life, scripture does more than simply leave us in this anxiety-ridden limbo. Three coping strategies are given: (1) focus on Christ, (2) be honest, and (3) rebel against sin.

Focus on Christ. I have described the complexity and variety of sin, but sin is not to be our focus. Christ is to be the focus of our attention. As we experience Christ, we continually grow to be more like him. For example, if we take seriously his acceptance of society's outcasts, we, too, find courage to show grace and sensitivity to people society would just as soon forget. As we focus on him, we are empowered by the Holy Spirit. His Spirit is given to us as a guarantee of future life and as the means for effective living. Even while we are at the same time saint and sinner, the Spirit is present with us to lead us continually closer to God.

Be honest. We need to be ruthlessly honest with

ourselves, with God, and with each other. Honesty requires that we be suspicious about ourselves, our motives, our desires—to face squarely that we are inverted around ourselves. We are all too ready to go it on our own, ignoring that God exists. Nowhere is that more likely to happen than with our money. With no difficulty we can allocate our finances to meet our "needs" without ever acknowledging God's claims on our resources.

I am convinced that truth is the most important ingredient for successful living. Confession is merely telling the truth about ourselves, and worship is telling the truth about God and what he has done in Christ. By affirming that we are both saint and sinner, we face the reality of our lives.

Honesty, however, includes much more than confession of sin and a discussion of our standing before God. Honesty requires that we admit that we are always tempted by pride and pleasure. We are capable of any sin. Honesty causes us to remember that we are temporary, that we brought nothing into this world and will take nothing out. Consequently, "things" are not life; Christ is.

Also, honesty requires that we view ourselves as God views us. If God says that we have new life in Christ, can we say less? The determining factor in our lives is not our sinfulness, but our new standing before God. We live always by and in his grace. That is the truth.

Rebel against sin. We ought not think of ourselves as wandering aimlessly between sin and right living. We ought not give in to sin as if it is inevitable or acceptable. It is not acceptable and we do not have to give in to it! For example, it would be easy for us to say "Nobody's perfect; all people lie a little to protect themselves, and therefore, it won't hurt if I bend the truth to save face." But each time that happens, we destroy ourselves a little. Sin is not to be tolerated.

When Paul discusses Christian living in Romans 6:12–14, he calls for rebellion against the tyranny of sin: "Do not let sin reign in your mortal body so that you obey its desires. Do not present the parts of your body to sin. . . . For sin will not lord it over you." Sin no longer has the right to rule over us, and we should not let it. Rather, as people who have just been raised from the dead and are looking around for something to do, we should present ourselves to God for service. Being a Christian is a change of lordships. Sin is no longer lord; Christ is!

We cannot get away from our sin, but in Christ we are also saints—God's people whom he has called and given his Spirit. We are at the same time saint and sinner, but we are to be determined by the former, not the latter.

Understanding Ourselves

4 Pride and Humility

In his youth General George Patton, the World War II hero, wrote of his intense desire to be great. He even said he would be willing to endure torture or die tomorrow, if for one day he could be great. What drives a man to seek such recognition of superiority? Is it pride or is it a fear of being shown to be inferior? Saul, Israel's first king, felt so inferior he tried to hide among some baggage to avoid being appointed king. Later he became so arrogant and jealous that he was almost insane. As Alfred Adler said, "To be human is to feel oneself inferior." Pride is the tool we use to block out the feelings of inferiority and give ourselves value.

Teenagers have the ability to look in the mirror and exclaim, "I am the greatest," and then twenty minutes later moan, "I am worthless." As it turns out, we never really lose this skill. We may become more sophisticated in our self-expression, but we find that we still give voice to both beliefs.

Few areas of tension are more obvious than that of pride and humility. Both words have positive and negative connotations. We know that pride is the essence of sin, and yet we also know that we should take pride in our achievements and in ourselves. Humility is considered a laudable virtue worthy of saints, but the word conjures up unappealing images of a self-effacing person "groveling in the dust."

But as we saw with *saint* and *sinner*, we cannot trust popular opinion on these matters. A biblical understanding of *pride* and *humility* gives us a less disjointed and more helpful perspective.

Pride, Foolishness, and Boasting

The most egotistical person I ever knew was a man named Jason. He could never work under anyone else because he felt he was superior to everyone. He had to be in control. More than once he felt he knew more than his college professors and disrupted class. He would not admit mistakes. Mistakes were what other people made. He once walked three miles out of his way rather than admit he was wrong about the location of a store. Instruction or constructive criticism from others were out of the question. He was a master at putting other people down. Everywhere he went he caused disunity and conflict. If he were being run out of town, he would have tried to make you think that he was leading a parade. The main problem for Jason was that no one else shared his high opinion of himself. His pride was blind and dumb. The only person deceived was himself.

What is the origin of pride? Pride emerges from the legitimate and necessary desire to show that our lives have value. That is why we use the word positively, for example, in saying we take "pride" in our work. We mean that we have shown we can *do* something of value. Pride becomes twisted, however, because we think that a personal asset or accomplishment gives *us* more value. Pride is the result of our thinking that our concerns, desires, and accomplishments are more important than those of other people. Like the disciples of Jesus who kept asking "Who is the greatest?" (Luke 22:24), we are not content with value, but desire superiority. Pride is no longer a feeling of accomplishment, but an estimation of ourselves as more valuable than someone else. Life then becomes dominated by the attempt to prop up that estimation.

Pride was a major problem in the church at Corinth. In fact, pride had led to divisions within the church. The Corinthian Christians were boasting about knowledge and spirituality. They were also attaching themselves to specific ministers as the hero of their group. People were saying, "I am of Paul," or "I am of Apollos," or "I am of Cephas," or even "I am of Christ." These arguments were about at the level of classic playground fights about whose father was the greatest. People also made exaggerated claims of knowledge and argued about who was "really" spiritual, which led to abuses of Christian freedom.

In his first letter to the Corinthians, Paul addresses these divisions. In summing up his argument he states:

> Let no one deceive himself. If anyone among you considers himself to be wise in this age, let that person become a fool in order that he may be wise. For the wisdom of this world is foolishness with God, for it is written, "God is the one who catches the wise in their conniv-

ing," and again, "The Lord knows the reason-
ings of the wise that they are worthless." So
then let no one boast in people, for all things
are yours, whether Paul or Apollos or Cephas
or the world or life or death or things present
or things future; all things are yours, and you
are Christ's and Christ is God's. (3:18–23)

The purpose of these surprising words is to help the
Corinthians arrive at a proper self-understanding as
Christians. The message is that we should neither
overestimate what we are nor should we underestimate
what we are in Christ.

"Let no one deceive himself." Pride is really a form
of self-deception. We are deluded when we attempt to
find meaning or purpose for life in ourselves or other
humans as if we were wise or could provide such a
foundation. And that was what the Corinthian Christians were up to. In essence they were fighting over who
was the wisest. They were deluded because anything
human is by its nature finite, temporary, and partial.

Pride invites this delusion. It looks within for its
foundation—for something it can comfortably rest
upon. It values accomplishments, friends, possessions,
abilities, and even spiritual gifts as factors that make a
person worthwhile and grant status. But Paul punctures
this fragile bubble. He points out that human wisdom is
inherently flawed. In fact, the wisdom of this world is
really foolishness. It is an attempt to ascribe ultimate
value to that which is partial and temporary.

Thus, Paul recommends that instead of clinging to
human wisdom, we are to become fools. Paul is not
simply singing the praise of folly or calling us to sacrifice
our intellects. Rather, he is urging us to perceive that the

"foolishness of God" is displayed in the cross. When Paul asks that we become fools, he means we become a fool from this world's perspective by identifying with the cross of Christ.

Mother Teresa is a good example of such a fool. She and her Missionaries of Charity walk the streets of Calcutta and bring back those who are dying. Their "house" is not a hospital but more of a hospice—a place to die with dignity. It is true that some recipients of their care improve and are even cured. But the main work is to care for the terminally ill patients. Many think this is foolish. Surely it would be wiser to devote the same energy and devotion instead to those who have a chance to be cured. Why waste time on those already slated to die when there are more deserving patients? It is here that Mother Teresa follows the way of the cross, stubbornly insisting that even the poorest of the poor who are dying are God's children and thus possess infinite value and are especially deserving of love and care.

The cross makes no sense from a merely human viewpoint. It is a sign of weakness, rejection, and failure. (See 1 Cor. 1:18–31.) But what seems like foolishness on God's part is actually the destruction of this world's wisdom. Real wisdom and power are to be found in God's saving activity in Christ. To identify with the cross of Christ is to refuse to find meaning and purpose solely in ourselves or in our accomplishments or in anything that is merely human. And this refusal is not a one-time decision; it is *a way of life*. Things that could be considered a means of gain are to be considered loss so that we might gain Christ (see Phil. 3:7).

Paul's immediate conclusion is that no one should boast in people (3:21). The various groups in Corinth were boasting in their adopted leaders such as Paul, Apollos, or Cephas (1:12). We, too, have our rallying points that end up being reasons for boasting and causes of division: "I am of Luther," "I am of Calvin," "I am of Wesley," "I am of Aquinas," or even "I am of Wimber." The thought that our association with some person, denomination, or movement makes us more significant is rather juvenile, but it is still common. People find their value in the fact that their worship is charismatic or free or liturgical or because their theology is conservative or moderate instead of liberal.

Despite Paul's concern to prevent boasting about Christian leaders, elsewhere he speaks of *legitimate* boasting. Quoting Jeremiah 9:24, Paul writes, "Let the one who boasts boast in the Lord" (1 Cor. 1:31). God's salvation precluded human boasting. You cannot boast about anything human, but you can "boast in the Lord."

Much of Paul's "boasting" theology is lost because translations often use a word like "rejoice" for those places where Paul uses the word *boasting* positively (see Rom. 5:2–3, 11). He rejected any attempt to boast "in the flesh," meaning in anything that is merely human. But he eagerly boasted about a variety of things the Lord has done. For example, he boasted in the cross (Gal. 6:14), the future glory of God and his present working in afflictions (Rom. 5:2–3), and the willingness of the Corinthians to assist monetarily (2 Cor. 9:2). Christians are even referred to as those who boast in Christ Jesus and have no confidence in the flesh (Phil. 3:3).

Similarly, Paul rejected a negative idea of commending himself (2 Cor. 3:1; 5:12; 10:12, 18), but he had a positive view of self-commendation in view of what God accomplished in or through him (2 Cor. 4:2; 6:4; 7:11).

So what can we conclude about pride? There is a legitimate drive for us to do acts of value, but neither those acts nor any assets we possess give us value. We must reject the whole process of trying to find true value in ourselves. Only God has abiding significance and value. Therefore, the only legitimate foundation for boasting is God and his activity in Christ. We overestimate what we are to our own peril. In doing so, we turn from that which has real value to an illusion.

True Humility

On the other hand, there is also a danger in underestimating what we are in Christ. Self-depreciation is just as much a problem as pride. On hearing that our righteous acts are like "filthy rags" (Isa. 64:6), people too often conclude that they are of no value. Knowing that pride is sin, we have driven ourselves into the arms of a false humility that is really self-effacement.

Tricia considers herself worthless and incapable of accomplishing anything significant. She does not feel that she deserves respect or decent treatment. Has her "humility" caused her to enjoy the fruits of righteousness? No. She married a man who mistreats her, and she is trapped in a miserable situation. True, she has rejected pride, but she has devalued herself in the process.

Few words are so poorly understood as *humility,* and few of us know how to practice it. We might well heed the words of Golda Meir: "Don't be so humble; you are not that great."

In our attempts to be humble we have ended up telling lies about ourselves, saying we cannot do things that we certainly can do well. Why would a corporate executive feel that he cannot pray in public? Why would a well-educated nurse feel that she could not learn about scripture and contribute meaningfully to the adults in her church? Our attempts at humility have led to self-effacement to the extent that we are unable to receive compliments. Our most common reaction to a compliment is to deny its validity.

The biblical concept of humility is not self-effacement and is not the least conducive to a "worm theology"—although the Bible does sometimes seem to give this impression: "I am just a worm and not a man" (Ps. 22:6). But humanity is viewed in a negative light only when seen as independent of God. Under those circumstances, the words of Isaiah 40:6–7 are correct: "All humans are like grass, and all their attractiveness is like the flowers of the field. The grass withers and the flowers fall." We are temporary and fleeting.

But we are also created in the image of God and *given* inestimable value through God's work of creation and redemption. The words of Psalm 8:4–5 recognize this aspect of our worth: "What is man that you are mindful of him or the son of man that you care for him? You have made him a little lower than the heavenly beings and crowned him with glory and honor." We are insignificant when viewed apart from God, but when viewed in relation to God we possess extreme value. That is why false humility is just as erroneous as pride: Both view our existence from a merely human viewpoint.

Rather than showing false humility, Paul makes several exalted claims about Christians throughout his letters. If we confine our attention only to the early chapters of 1 Corinthians, we find that we have received "the Spirit which is from God" (2:12); we have "the mind of Christ" (2:16); we are "God's temple" (3:16);

we were "washed," "sanctified," and "declared righteous in the name of the Lord Jesus Christ and by the Spirit of our God" (6:11). There is no self-effacement here! On the contrary, these words represent the value that has been given to people by the grace of God in Christ.

The most surprising of such statements, however, is the one made in 1 Corinthians 3:21–23: "All things are yours, whether Paul or Apollos or Cephas or the world or life or death or things present or things future; all things are yours, and you are Christ's and Christ is God's."

Could Paul have really meant "All things are yours"? His initial concern was to explain that the Corinthians do not belong to their ministers; rather, their ministers belong to them. But the passage moves far beyond the gift of ministers to the church. He goes on to say that not only do Paul, Apollos, and Cephas belong to them, but also the world, life, death, the present, and the future belong to those in Christ. That is quite a gift!

These realities are no longer to threaten or control us. Rather, they are to be owned and appropriated for life in Christ. Even the world and death are ours to be used for God. That to which we instinctively cling, such as life itself and the present, and that which we instinctively dread or look forward to are no longer realities that dominate us or determine who we are. There is a larger reality, life in Christ, in which every other fact or event is enclosed and by which it is shaped and empowered. All things are ours in Christ. In him humanity discovers its lost lordship. Here is the basis for freedom and a foundation for life.

Ryan White, the Indiana schoolboy, knew for years that he was dying of AIDS. Yet, during the controversy over his not being allowed to attend school and the ensuing press coverage, many people marveled at the calm demeanor and infectious humor with which he lived. He expressed a confidence in God that took the terror out of death and allowed him to live freely, even with the monstrous cruelty of AIDS.

Paul did not fear death either. Nor was the world for him something to possess or fear. Rather, Paul felt all things were his, including death and the world, to be used in service for Christ. For Christians, in a real sense, the world is our oyster. Self-effacement has no legitimate place in our lives.

Obviously, Paul's words are open to abuse. They could easily be taken out of context and made the basis for a kind of "triumphalism" of which Christians have too often been guilty. In triumphalism the focus is placed so heavily on victory that the reality of sin and failure is ignored. "God has promised to make me wealthy, healthy, and happy." Sadly, these attitudes invariably lead to pride and even to the denigration of others. Triumphalism is another instance of emphasizing the new age to such an extent that the reality of the old age and the "not yet" aspects of our faith are forgotten.

What is surprising about our text, however, is that Paul made these "all-is-yours" statements to the church in Corinth, the very church guilty of triumphalism. We cannot correct the error of triumphalism by diminishing the victory of Christ or the privileges available in him. All things *are* ours in Christ.

But triumphalism does need correcting, and Paul does just that. First, while it appears that Paul has given the Corinthians a basis for their boasting, really he has pulled the carpet out from under all boasting. He told them, "All things are yours," but added, "And you are

Christ's and Christ is God's." Only as we are Christ's are all things ours. Our possession of all things is determined by Christ and our relation to him. Certainly that prevents any abuse resulting from egotism or ideas of privilege.

Second, to be Christ's is to be shaped by both his death and resurrection. Triumphalism forgets what the Corinthians had forgotten, the cross of Jesus Christ. The content of Paul's gospel centered on the resurrection *and* the cross. While the resurrection dominates the end of the letter, the cross dominates the beginning (see especially 1:23 and 2:2). The statement "All things are yours" is couched in a theology of the cross. The willingness to give ourselves in identification with the Crucified One excludes selfishness and individualism. All things are ours to be used in service to Christ.

The attempt to avoid abuse of Paul's words should not diminish our appreciation of the breadth and depth of what we receive in Christ. Similar expressions of value occur throughout Paul's letters and the rest of the Bible: Christians are fellow heirs with Christ, members of God's family, glorified with Christ, given the glory that God gave Christ, and given the Holy Spirit. Such expressions could be multiplied easily. The point is that we have received value and standing by God's grace in Christ. There is no limit to the grace that has been given to us. But as always with grace, there is also a call to responsibility. Life has not only been given to us, but meaning and purpose have been given, too, in the call to serve the one we now affirm as Lord.

True humility, therefore, is that which recognizes that our meaning, purpose, talents, abilities, and even our life are not our own but are gifts received from a gracious God.

Beyond Pride and False Humility

In the Christian life there is simply no room for either
pride or self-effacement. The choice left to us is not a
tightrope walk between the two, but an entirely different
kind of life.

Pride and false humility share a common perspective: Both see the self as an isolated entity, but grace
moves us to a new horizon with a new perspective. Now
we see ourselves in relationship with God in Christ. The
wealth this relationship brings, however, is no basis for
pride. It is the wealth of a steward, not of an owner. In
1 Corinthians 4:7 Paul asks the pointed question,
"What do you have that you did not receive? And if you
received it, why are you boasting as if you did not?"

We cannot ignore who we are or what we have, and
we are not asked to. We are asked, however, to find the
basis of life in God rather than in ourselves and to know
that whatever we are or have is a gift of God's grace.

Having a proper self-understanding did not stop
Paul from having a very robust view of the importance
of his ministry. He took a back seat to no one. (Read,
for example, Gal. 1–2, Rom. 15, or 1 Cor. 3–4.) On
the other hand, Paul referred to himself as the least of
the saints (Eph. 3:8) and as the least of the apostles
because he had persecuted the church (1 Cor. 15:9).
But even his persecution of the church did not lead to
self-depreciation, for he went on to make one of the
most freeing statements ever made: *"By the grace of God I
am what I am,* and his grace to me has not been without
effect" (1 Cor. 15:10).

Our defects and failures are not causes for self-
depreciation, and our strengths and accomplishments are
not the basis for pride. All we are, we are by God's grace.

This is the basis of our freedom, service, and unity. Grace should never be used as an excuse for us to do nothing; it is an excuse for just the opposite! We are responsible to see that grace has its effect in our lives.

The best teacher I ever knew was a man whom one would not expect to be able to speak publicly at all. Mr. Hatch was a quiet, almost bashful man—more likely choosing to be in a corner by himself than behind a podium. He told our class once that he would have been happy to be an elevator operator on the college campus. But God's call would not allow him to be self-effacing. By grace and with hard work Mr. Hatch developed knowledge, insight, and an ability to communicate in a way that was spellbinding. That ability did not make him better than other people, and he did not act as if he thought he were. He became for me a prime example of humility—competent and gifted because he trusted God, worked hard, and let none of his accomplishments go to his head.

As Mr. Hatch had learned, our self-understanding must be derived from our relation to God. We should not overestimate our own importance as if we were the center of the universe and all things revolved around us. By ourselves, we are nothing, a soon-to-be-wilted flower. On the other hand, we should not underestimate ourselves, for we have been given "all things" by our relationship to God. To borrow Paul's words, we can do all things through Christ who strengthens us.

Blaise Pascal expressed our tension this way:

> The knowledge of God without that of man's misery causes pride. The knowledge of man's misery without that of God causes despair. The knowledge of Jesus Christ constitutes the

middle course, because in him we find both God and our misery. Jesus Christ is a God whom we may approach without pride, and before whom we humble ourselves without despair. (*Pensées*, 526–27)

Give up trying to be superior and be faithful instead. Reject messages of inferiority, even internal ones; grace says that it does not matter. By the grace of God, we are what we are! That is a proper self-understanding and a foundation for meaningful life.

Understanding Ourselves

5 Strength and Weakness

Elliot liked to play baseball in the street with his friends. But when it came time to try out for Little League, he feared he would do poorly, so he did not try out. In time his friends learned to play better, but Elliot never did. Rather than risk the possibility of looking incompetent, he gave up the sport he enjoyed.

We will do almost anything to avoid being viewed as incompetent or weak. Revealing that we cannot do something makes us feel small and inferior. So we try to avoid our areas of weakness. But we cannot. Life laughingly taunts us, "Are you competent for this?" and hands us a new challenge. Playing baseball may not be an area of insecurity for you, but we all have one.

Society has taught us ways of "looking" competent, especially if we belong to the middle or upper classes. Most of us can look competent by wearing the right clothes, saying the right things most of the time, and avoiding bad manners. But these are only appearances, a veneer. We still have feelings of weakness and insecurity, and we encounter various kinds of failure.

We are driven to prove ourselves strong and competent, and we should, for God has created us to be capable. At the same time, our capabilities are limited, and life sometimes appears to be too big a challenge. We need to prove ourselves, but we are also afraid of failure. We are always vulnerable to failure, and as we age, vulnerability increases. We know we have limitations, but God seems to call us past our limitations. Jeremiah complained that he was too young to be a prophet and could not speak, but God called him anyway. We are caught between the fear of failure and the need to prove, between awareness of our weakness and God's call to serve with strength.

Men, in particular, often hide their weakness by showing how tough they are. Sometimes women attempt the same tactic. Proving how tough we are may seem necessary in a "dog-eat-dog" world, but it destroys our ability to be sensitive and to have meaningful relationships. A "don't tread on me" attitude does not invite intimacy or trust.

The Bible ultimately is about competent living. Like Joshua, we are called to be strong and courageous (1:6). Whether through laws, proverbs, parables, or promises, the Bible in effect says, "This is the way; walk in it and please God." But what the Bible has to say about competent living is sometimes disconcerting. For instance, in 2 Corinthians 12:10 we read, "When I am weak, then I am strong." Once again we are confronted with the fact that scripture's point of view is dramatically opposed to human common sense. Misunderstanding of the dynamics of strength and weakness is rampant even among Christians.

Jim and Nancy lived in Atlanta where Jim had a very good job and a bright future. Nancy was offered the editorial job she wanted in Louisville. Should Jim display "strength" and insist they stay in Atlanta? Or should he show "weakness" by being willing to move?

Gretchen betrayed Tom by taking several real estate clients from him. Should he show "strength" and seek revenge, or should he be "weak" and forgive her?

As with pride and humility, *strength* and *weakness* can be viewed positively or negatively. *Strength* may point to competence and to the power of God working in us, but it can also be used of the illusion that we are strong enough on our own. *Weakness* may point to our inadequacies or human limitations, but, as we will see, it can be used positively to refer to identification with the cross of Christ.

Just as we found that in the biblical treatment of pride and humility the way up is down, so, too, we will find here that the biblical formula for strength is found in giving it up.

Am I Weak or Am I Strong?

Of the several words for "man" in biblical Hebrew, two of them seem to have opposite connotations. One appears to derive from a root with the meaning "strong," and the other from a root suggesting "weakness."

Both connotations are true of human beings, depending on how we look at things. But neither approach, viewed by itself, is valid.

Misunderstanding prevents competent living. Either we overestimate or undervalue our capabilities. Some people reduce the words of Philippians 4:13, "I can do all things in the one empowering me," to, "I can do all things." Their attitude is that they can handle life—with or without God. We tend to be aware of God only when we need him. Then having used all the right language about God, we presumptuously expect him to do our bidding. But God does not work that way.

The truth is that none of us is competent for all of life. We deceive ourselves by ignoring our frailty and limitations. We have forgotten the words of Jesus: "Apart from me you can do nothing" (John 15:5). We can live a life that looks competent, but competent living does not come from our attempts to prove competence and hide incompetence. In the final analysis, we have only avoided the areas of weakness and difficulty. Without God any competence we have—even though it is itself a gift from God—is limited and temporary.

Other people make the opposite error. They take Jesus' words, "Apart from me you can do nothing," and abbreviate them to, "I can do nothing." Too many people view themselves as weak and incompetent.

Jesus' words do not imply that those without Christ cannot accomplish anything. It is quite obvious that those who do not know Christ can be creative, productive, wise, helpful, loving, and capable in many areas. Bearing fruit is the subject under discussion in John 15. What the text means is that no person can accomplish anything in connection with the purposes of Christ apart from Christ.

The text does not mean that we are inherently incapable and weak, but amazingly that is exactly what a good number of people, especially Christians, say about themselves. Nothing is more devastating to competent living—to authentic relations, to love, to learning, and to productivity—than a negative self-image.

The truth is that we are both weak and strong. We live with both realities.

Getting Rid of Incompetence

Chet never got any breaks in life. His home situation was not good, and he did not do well in school. Although actually a quite capable person, he felt he had few options in life beyond the very ordinary. He could not imagine being useful to God. Too many people are like Chet. Although they might not say so, they view themselves as incompetent.

A negative self-image results in self-doubt and in a fear of people and situations. Faced with a task or opportunity, people can become so shackled with fear that they cannot do the job before them. One recourse is simply not to do the work, so as to avoid the risk involved, or follow the strategy that a friend once described as his custom: "I always fight with one hand behind my back so that if I lose I have an excuse." How many "battles" are lost unnecessarily on such approaches?

Christians often further confuse the situation by misapplying the words of 2 Corinthians 12:9: "My grace is sufficient for you, for power is perfected in weakness." We try to turn our deficiencies into virtues, but it will not work. When Paul refers to weaknesses, he does not mean incompetence. The context of this verse points to Paul's "thorn in the flesh," probably some physical malady that cannot be identified. Other texts where Paul speaks of weakness refer to Paul's suffering for the gospel in his missionary efforts (2 Cor. 11:30) or to his identification with the cross of Christ (2 Cor. 13:4). Weakness does not refer to incompetence; it refers to the difficulties encountered in living and proclaiming the gospel.

Paul placed no value on his accomplishments or standing in his community. Rather, he considered all things as loss to gain Christ (Phil. 3:4–8). However, it is one thing to refuse to place value on accomplishments or standing, and it is quite another to have no accomplishments or standing.

Three factors render people incompetent. First, they fight the wrong battles. They put all their energy and time in figuring out more and more elaborate ways for not facing the very area they need to confront. This is merely a "defense mechanism" to avoid the truth. It is like worrying whether your paper clips are in order instead of dealing with the tough issues of your job. Churches worry about their organizational structure and programs and never get around to expressing and living the gospel. Life must be focused on issues and problems that really count. To live competently requires the wisdom to determine what needs to be done and the honesty to deal with it directly.

Second, some people are incompetent because they are not willing to expend the energy required to succeed. They are too passive and lazy. Pascal commented that pride and laziness are the twin sources of all vices (*Pensées*, 435). He added that the gospel drives both out. It is impossible to serve God and be lazy.

Third, some people are rendered incompetent because others have convinced them that they are incompetent. People were not born with self-doubts. They were taught along the way. These people were given a negative self-image by abuse (whether sexual, physical, or emotional) or neglect. They were not given the grace and help needed to learn to be what God had called them to be.

A friend of mine, whose father rejected him from day one, is a very capable individual The father even accused the hospital of giving him and his wife the wrong baby. All his life the son was described by his father as "dumb," and after a while the boy began to believe it. He is just as capable as anyone else, but he may never fully recover from the damage done to him by his father. Thankfully, the grace of God can work to heal such scars, but it requires time and it requires a place where grace can be encountered.

The only way out of such a quagmire of self-doubt is to begin to take seriously one of the first things we learn from reading scripture: that it was God who created us, that he declared his creation good, and that he created us in his image. God does not create incompetence. We are competent enough. We have the value and abilities God created us to have. That does not mean we can do anything we wish, nor does it mean that we all are equally capable. People do have varying levels of ability. But we can focus on the tasks appropriate to God's leading, and we can work to prepare ourselves to perform those tasks. And so, by God's grace, we show ourselves to be competent.

One of the privileges granted me is the opportunity to teach Greek to seminarians. Nothing puts the fear of failure into people as quickly as the requirement to take Greek. Students allow themselves to become mesmerized because they have heard all their lives of things not understood, "It's Greek to me." Biblical Greek in particular is not difficult, especially since there are numerous helps available. Actually, there are only two problems to overcome in learning Greek: the fear people bring with them and their lack of knowledge of English. Discipline is required, but that is true of any learning. Such tasks as learning Greek are not beyond the capability of most people if they put forth the necessary effort and do not fight the wrong battles.

Whether for Greek or for any other part of life, one must *want* to perform competently and must be willing to face the risk of failure. No success was ever attained without the risk of failure. But failure is not nearly as bad as we suspect. Grace even allows us room to fail and start over and try again. Much more dreadful than failure is the fear that shackles us and either keeps us from trying or hobbles our efforts.

The Source of Competence

So far we have determined that first, people erroneously see themselves as the source of competence; second, people are deceived when they see themselves as incompetent. Some readers may conclude that I am speaking out of both sides of my mouth, but, in fact, both statements are true—though neither is adequate by itself.

The solution is not a balancing act between viewing ourselves as sometimes strong and sometimes weak. Even when we are strong and competent, then we are weak. Our strength is temporary at best, and often an illusion. There is a necessary tension between the affirmation of strength and the confession of weakness. But both statements are inadequate because they both make the same error: They view the individual merely as an isolated self.

Paul said, "When I am weak, then I am strong." How can weakness be strength? But Paul was not talking about human strength. What appears to be human strength is actually weakness, for it is an attempt to promote and defend oneself. Weakness is true strength because focus on the self is removed. No longer is the self promoted and defended. Rather, the "weak" person is willing to spend him or herself, to let go, and let God work. It is a way of identifying with the cross of Christ. True strength is what God is able to accomplish through us. When we are willing to be weak enough not to focus on ourselves, then the Spirit of God can work through us to accomplish the purposes of God.

We need to be as capable as possible, but not so we can further our own interests and look competent. Rather, we are to be as capable as possible so that we may identify with the weakness of Christ's giving himself for others. That is true strength.

Whether strong or weak, we are not to understand those terms in isolation from God. We were not created to be viewed any other way than in relation to God. He is the one who is the source of any strength or ability that we have, whether through creation or through a life of faith. God is also the source of our strength through the Spirit given to us at redemption. Our weaknesses are known and ministered to by God. God is the one who makes us competent.

God often uses those who think themselves incompetent to do great deeds. In Exodus 3 we witness Moses trying his best to convince God that he had chosen the wrong deliverer for Israel. John the Baptist claimed that he was not competent even to carry the Messiah's sandals (Matt. 3:11). Paul confessed that he was not competent to be called an apostle because he had persecuted the church (1 Cor. 15:9). But the confession of human incapacity is not the end of these discussions.

Human incapacity was, and continues to be, subsumed under God's capacities.

Paul deals with this dynamic tension in his second letter to the Corinthians. After describing the character of Christian ministry, he asks, "Who is competent for such tasks?" (2:16). His answer is, "We are," but with some qualifications: "We have such confidence through Christ before God. Not that we are competent from ourselves to claim anything as from ourselves, but our competence comes from God. He has made us competent as ministers of a new covenant" (3:4–6).

Our competency is given to us from God. Significantly, the translators of the Hebrew Old Testament into Greek used the *Competent One* as a name for God. He alone is competent, and in him we find our competency for the life he has given us.

This is not to suggest that our relationship to God will automatically give us strength and competency, as if at conversion God touches people with a magic wand. Natural abilities and preferences for specific tasks will in most cases still be present, even though they may change over the years. Competency will still depend on training, great effort, and the application of a wisdom that is grounded in Christ. Competency does not just happen; it is honed through great effort in the hands of God. Martin Luther was a marvelously competent Christian leader, but not just because he was willing to be a leader. He was well-taught and he worked strenuously at translating, writing, preaching, and teaching as he sought to do God's will with God's assistance.

Finding one's competency in God will require vulnerability and a willingness to be led and empowered. It will require a willingness to be made weak in identification with the cross. Such vulnerability and willingness are made easier for those of us who have found freedom and grace. We do not have to prove our toughness. We do not have to fear that we will be found incompetent. Christ has shown us that the only way to find life is to lose it.

Dietrich Bonhoeffer knew this when he returned to Germany in 1939 rather than stay in the United States where he would be safe. His return allowed him to minister to his people, but it resulted in his arrest and execution. On a more ordinary plane, a church loses life to find it by graciously receiving the outcasts of society, such as people with AIDS. Christians experience this when they give up leisure time to instruct others or to work with Habitat for Humanity, with soup kitchens, or ministering to the handicapped. People lose life and find it when, as service to God, they sacrifice desires and pleasures to enable family members to succeed.

God has made his people capable servants of his new covenant. They are competent for worship, ministry, witness, giving, patience, grief, suffering, work, and rejoicing.

But the question arises as to what part of the process is the divine part and what part is the human. If God is the source for our competency, how do we distinguish who is responsible for what in our activities? As popular as these questions are, they are misguided. We cannot separate God's activity from the activity of his people. God works in and through people. We must stop viewing ourselves as isolated individuals. Rather, we must see ourselves in union with God. He works through us, not on us. We can no more separate God's part and our part than we can separate the divine and human natures of Christ.

Once again the thoughts of Blaise Pascal provide a

fitting summary of the tension with which we have been dealing:

> I see everywhere nothing but obscurities. Am I to believe that I am nothing? Am I to believe that I am God? ... The true religion should teach greatness and wretchedness, should make us both respect and scorn the self, love and hate it.... There is nothing on earth which does not reveal either the wretchedness of man [sic], or the mercy of God; or the power-lessness of man without God, or the strength of man with God. (*Pensées*, 227, 494, 561)

Understanding Ourselves

6 Authority and Submission

Once while visiting a church, I was confronted with what I thought was a remarkable situation. It seems that some of the women in this church refused to take responsibility for anything they did wrong. The church had been heavily influenced by the teachings of Christian speaker Bill Gothard, who emphasizes the authority of God and men, and the submission of women and unmarried children. Therefore, these women reasoned that their husbands were to blame for any wrong they as wives had done, since they were under their husbands' "umbrella" of authority!

This is an unusual expression of what has become a hotly debated subject within the church: that is, the proper roles of authority and submission.

The opposite extreme is also represented: those who reject authority entirely. I cannot forget a discussion I had with a cynical young woman. She was so tired of the abuse of authority that she could not imagine legitimate authority. She even balked at calling Jesus "Lord," preferring instead to call him "Friend."

How we relate to authority is one of the most important issues in life. Teenagers and parents tussle over control. Problems in school or at work are frequently problems of authority. A faculty member at a school in the South complained that his school could not have faculty as heads of departments, for no one could be entrusted with that much authority. Problems in churches are usually, at bottom, problems of authority. I know of an effective pastor who quit his church because the lay leaders argued only they could make decisions about the church. Conversely, at another church the pastor was forced to resign because he had insisted that the church had to do what he said. These examples are not extreme.

Yet, despite their importance, we seldom discuss openly the subjects of authority and submission. Either we are afraid of confronting such strong differences of opinion, or we are too uncomfortable with the words themselves. We merely avoid the issues.

But we can avoid authority and submission about as easily as we can avoid breathing. Every social organization, including the church, is made up of an intricate web of authority and submission.

Authority: A Necessary Evil?

What does *authority* really mean? Good definitions are hard to come by. I have a friend who objects to women in positions of authority over men. When asked to define *authority,* he replied, "I don't know what it is, but women can't have it." An adequate definition just might make us rethink some of our arguments.

When we speak of authority, we are referring to *the communication of power to achieve a particular belief or action by others.* This power might be expressed by example and reasoned argument, as with Jesus, or it might be expressed by coercive force, as with Pilate. It might be something as simple as a mother explaining how the toothpaste ought to be squeezed or as complex as the president running a nation. But in each case someone is exercising some type of power, whether rightly or wrongly, to affect the behavior of others.

There are various kinds of authority: authority based on knowledge, on physical force, on charismatic attraction, on position, or on financial clout. Authority may be shared so that it is exercised by various people at different times, or it may be limited to a select few. But wherever people are together, power is being communicated, and therefore authority is being exercised.

In addition to *power,* legitimate authority contains a second component: the idea of *right.* When authority is valid, it has the right to exercise power. We need both aspects of authority: right and power. The problem is that too often we find those who have the right but not the power, and those who have the power but not the right. The first results in inept leadership; the latter results in abusive leadership.

However we express it, we all exercise some form of authority. We may not be someone else's boss, but we have responsibility for other people, which requires the communication of authority. Parents have authority—for good or ill. Teachers have authority—whether the teaching is formal or informal, and all of us teach much more frequently than we are aware. When we drive a car or run some type of machine we are expressing a kind of authority. We cannot escape authority—our own or that of others, and there is nothing inherently evil in it. Without authority there is anarchy.

But authority does get abused. In this world, authority mixes with our sin and pride and gets expressed as, "I get to be boss. I am up; you are down. You have to submit to me and do what I say." The real dangers and abuses of authority come when it is viewed as a *personal possession.* "I have the authority; therefore I will do what I want. I am the one in control here. I don't have to listen to anyone." Such attitudes inevitably lead to disaster.

Even so, people often submit to such authority out of self-interest—if they are paid enough or if they feel they must submit to maintain order or preserve their own safety. Too often, authority and submission are both ways of seeking the best for ourselves in view of the circumstances.

A Different Kind of Authority

Contrary to what some people think, authority is not obliterated in Christianity. Jesus appointed twelve persons with special functions. The early church appointed elders, deacons, and a variety of other leaders. Where people lead and coordinate or take responsibility and accomplish tasks, authority is being expressed.

In Christ, however, authority is expressed and partaken of, but *it is never possessed.* Only the Triune God possesses authority. We may usurp authority or we may partake of God's authority, but only he possesses it.

The entire New Testament is concerned to show the authority of Jesus in his teaching, in his works, and in his exaltation over every authority and power. He gives similar authority to his disciples to continue his ministry.

All of Paul's letters either assume or seek to establish his authority over his churches. In Galatians and the Corinthian letters Paul had to defend the legitimacy of his apostolic authority. And yet Paul only twice used the word *authority* with reference to his ministry (2 Cor. 10:8 and 13:10). Why? Because Paul rightly believed that he did not possess authority in and of himself. He merely expressed authority and partook of it to the degree that he proclaimed the gospel. Consequently, when Paul defended his role as an apostle in Galatians and in the Corinthian letters, he focused on the gospel, his commission to preach, and the fact that his activity had been in character with the gospel.

We are not to snatch the right to lead nor do we control the power of the gospel. On the contrary, the gospel lays hold of us and directs our lives. All of us then have authority for life, but any authority we have is the authority of the gospel made available through us by our words and lives.

Thus, once again we find that in Christ we are moved to a different spectrum—this time to one where authority and submission function differently from how they function in the world. The authority of Christians is an authority *for* others and not an authority *over* others.

Any authority that we have—whether within the family, the church, in our occupations, or in society—is not ours but God's, and has been given to us for ministry. This perspective puts many "checks" on our expression of authority:

First, Christians should not claim authority in areas where they have neither the right nor the ability, since these are ways God leads us.

Second, there is no place within the body of Christ for being authoritarian, since our authority is not our own and because its expression should conform to Jesus' life and teaching.

Third, in Christ, authority does not lead to the denigration of people. If anything, it leads to a "denigration" of the one in authority, for that person is made the servant of others (see 1 Cor. 4:9–13). Authority does not push one person up and other people down, since we are all one in Christ (Gal. 3:28).

Fourth, our authority does not allow any room for pride or self-congratulation. Authority does not make us one bit better than we were without it.

Finally, and most important of all, authority is not a prize to be clutched or even sought after. The self-giving love of the Christ who did not consider equality with God something to be grasped (Phil. 2:6) will not allow his followers to be so enamored with status and position. They, too, must practice the same self-giving love.

The practice of authority that is really for others is far different from the authority we usually see. Such authority has no need to be defensive, and if wrongly attacked, defends itself by the character of the gospel. Such authority is quick to listen and recognize both the temporary character of its leadership and that the leadership is itself a gift of God's grace.

A person is not appointed chair of a church to enhance his or her ego. Like any leader, that person leads only by the permission of the people. The chairperson is to provide leadership and coordination to the congregation but can do that only by listening and enabling people to do their jobs. If that does not happen, the chairperson fails.

This is not true merely for church leaders. As Max De Pree argues in his book *Leadership Is an Art*, these

Christian principles are good business practices in the "secular" world.

Submission: Do I Have To?

To speak of authority, however, is to speak of only half of the issue. There can be no authority without a corresponding submission.

We all feel uncomfortable when we find the New Testament instructing us to submit. In fact, a recent scholarly work actually tried to argue that all the New Testament texts referring to submission were later additions that appeared sometime in the second century! Even if we do not like it, the gospel does not just ask some of us to submit to others; it asks that we *all* submit to each other in Christ.

Mutual submission does not make any sense by this world's view of things (where submission only takes place when a subordinate yields to a superior). In fact, even Christians have had difficulty with the idea of mutual submission. But the message of the Bible is clear. Christian living requires that we "submit to one another in reverence to Christ" (Eph. 5:21).

Submission is not the same as obedience or doing someone else's will, and it certainly is not weakness. Submission by Christians means *the voluntary surrender of one's rights or will in response to the purposes and actions of God.* Closely related are the ideas of humility and *agape* love, by which Christians are willingly to give themselves in love to others. Submission to each other is another way of identifying with the death of Christ. Thus, just as authority does not elevate, submission does not lower.

Jesus himself explains this radical thinking on authority and mutual submission in the gospel of Mark.

The brothers James and John had requested to sit at Jesus' right and left in his kingdom (positions of privilege and status), and the other disciples were angry—no doubt because they had not thought of it first. Jesus summoned them and said:

> You know that the ones regarded as rulers among the Gentiles lord it over them and their high officials dominate them. It is not this way with you. Whoever wishes to be great among you will be your servant, and whoever wishes to be first among you will be slave of all. For the Son of Man did not come to be served, but to serve and to give his life as a ransom for many. (10:42–45)

Here Jesus seems to be collapsing the categories of authority and submission. Authority is responsibility, and whoever has the most authority or responsibility will also have to practice the most submission. But Jesus' teaching raises some questions: How can a person lead if he or she always has to be submitting to everyone's requests? How can any of us submit when the actions or requests of the other person are wrong?

Submission does not mean that every request has to be honored. Nor should wrong be ignored or tolerated. Jesus certainly did not tolerate wrong or become a doormat acquiescing to every request. Yet at the same time, he was willing to submit to the point that he died on a cross.

The gospel directs that we submit to others as an act of love and service. Any act of submission that is not in accordance with the gospel's understanding of love and service is invalid. The same is true for the use of authority. The gospel views authority as an act of service for others. In fact, submission and authority both function as self-giving love for others.

Husbands and Wives

For many of us, the most important aspect of this issue is how authority and submission are to work in our marriages—especially, the Bible's teaching on the submission of wives to their husbands. Poor teaching in this area has caused much discomfort and has led to abuse of women.

Take Emily's situation, for example. Emily's alcoholic husband moved into a house down the street from her and came home only when he wanted a meal, sexual relations, or the laundry done. Should she submit to such treatment? Christian friends had told this woman that she had no other option than to submit. That is absurd! No woman has to submit to that kind of treatment. She (or a man in a similar situation) should show as much faithful love as possible. But giving in to such demands would be a sacrifice of integrity and would reinforce the husband's wrong way of life.

How should we understand the texts asking wives to submit to their husbands? Some argue for the authority and dominance of the male on biblical grounds. They use the Bible to keep women "in their place." Others disregard the texts on submission, saying they are cultural statements that no longer apply. Neither approach is valid. A more careful reading will show that the Bible's teaching is much more radical than we had thought.

In most of the ancient world in which the Bible was written, women were dominated by men in almost every respect. Most were denied the privileges of education.

They could not vote or act as witnesses in a court of law. They were often treated as sexual objects and were under the authority of their fathers, husbands, sons, or some other male relative. Their religious belief was usually determined by their husbands.

The actions of Jesus in accepting women and teaching them was striking. Similarly, the statements of the early church about women gave them new freedom that is hard for us to appreciate.

Some of the statements that seem negative to us were caused by women abusing their newfound freedom. Directions on conduct in the ancient world typically grouped wives, children, and slaves together. The statements in Ephesians 5 were all necessary to explain how household relationships were to be lived out in the new faith. In fact, Christianity was accused of destroying the family because it encouraged women not to take their husband's religion. They should be Christians even if their husbands were not (1 Cor. 7:15). Wives are asked to submit to their husbands as an indication that Christianity is not destructive of the family. As Titus 2:5 puts it, wives are to submit *so that* the word of God is not blasphemed.

The best-known text dealing with the submission of wives occurs in Ephesians 5:22. However, it is an error to begin reading at 5:22. We must start reading at least at 5:21 where the subject is mutual submission. In fact, in 5:22 the word *submit* is not even in the better Greek manuscripts; it is assumed from 5:21. The submission of wives can only be treated as a specific example of mutual submission that is asked of all Christians. Note that most of the attention in this text is not on the submission of the wives, but on the self-giving of the husbands:

Submit to each other in reverence to Christ. Wives, to your own husbands as to the Lord. For the husband is the head of the wife as Christ is the head of the church. . . . But as the church submits to Christ, so also wives should submit to their husbands in everything.

Husbands, love your wives, just as Christ loved the church and gave himself for her. . . . In the same way, husbands ought to love their wives as their own bodies. He who loves his wife loves himself. For no one ever hated his own body, but he nourishes and cares for it, just as Christ does the church—for we are members of his body. "For this reason a man will leave his father and mother and will be joined to his wife, and the two will become one flesh." (vv. 21–25, 28–31)

Here, and in most other texts addressing husband and wife relationships, we find statements that seem to support two different models: a hierarchical model in which the husband is the head of the wife, and an egalitarian model in which husband-wife equality is stressed.

In Ephesians 5 the egalitarian emphasis is in the focus on mutual submission and in the statement that the two will be one flesh. No matter what else is said, certainly the real head of both husband and wife is Christ. He is the Lord by whom both marriage partners order their lives together. The hierarchical emphasis is seen in the statement that the husband is head.

Neither the hierarchical nor the egalitarian models can be set aside by some exegetical wizardry. That certainly has been tried by both sides. Neither model can be viewed as normative while the other is only cultural or conditional. The egalitarian model cannot be viewed as unsuitable for a sinful world. The hierarchical cannot be dismissed on the grounds that "head" should be translated as "source," although the word in question is still heavily debated. Both the hierarchical and the egalitarian emphases remain.

To solve this alleged riddle, we must focus on two questions: First, why is the husband said to be the head of the wife? Second, what are the results if we understand male headship in light of the whole context?

Why is the husband said to be the head of the wife? The husband is called head because he is given responsibility for his wife to care for her and make sure that she is not abused. In this sinful world women have always been abused and are usually more vulnerable to a variety of types of abuse than men are. First Peter 3:7 refers to women as the "weaker vessel." That description is not intended to be pejorative. It is a reference to the fact that women tend to be weaker physically than men. This is not to suggest that women cannot train themselves for great physical accomplishments or that women cannot take care of themselves. It is simply a recognition that in this sinful world women tend to be more vulnerable than men and are abused more frequently. The concern is thus for the nurture and care of the wife. As we discovered earlier, the biblical model of authority is service *for* rather than *over* another.

Second, what are the results if we understand male headship in light of the whole context? The important point in focusing on mutual submission is that the husband's being head does not result in some position of privilege. It is a position of *responsibility* in which the husband is to love his wife and give himself for her, care for her, and nurture her (Eph. 5:25, 28–29). If the wife is asked to submit to the husband and the husband is asked to love and give himself for his wife, is the wife being asked to do more in submitting than the husband is in giving himself? I certainly do not know what it would be. In the new reality revealed by Christ, what the world sees as the polar opposites, authority and submission are collapsed together and work together in service and love for others.

In 1 Corinthians 7:3–4 Paul makes another radical claim (especially when one considers that he is writing in the first century). Paul states that the wife does not have authority over her body; rather the husband does. But he says the same thing about the husband: The wife has authority over his body. Marriage is to effect a union in which the two persons give themselves to each other. The responsibility of the husband to care for his wife receives greater emphasis, but the dynamic by which the two live as one is mutual submission. That is the way love operates.

Invariably the question is raised, "Don't you need someone to make the decision when there is disagreement, and isn't that the responsibility of the husband as head?"

The question seems impatient with the process that leads to unity and in the end is misguided. If Christ is the Lord of the home and leads both husband and wife, should unity be sacrificed for a decision? This is not to suggest that Christian husbands and wives always agree. But where mutual submission is being practiced and where the gospel is the basis of decisions, even where there is disagreement about an issue there should be unity and a workable solution. Mutual submission would allow that either person might make a decision in a given situation. Where a workable solution cannot be achieved, unless circumstances absolutely prohibit it, then both husband and wife should go back to the drawing board.

What Christ Expects

There are other subjects where the tension of authority and submission should be discussed. The relation of pastors and congregations and of governments and citizens are two obvious areas of potential abuse. But authority and submission function the same way here as elsewhere.

Mutual submission and legitimate authority expressed in the context of love and service are the goals. Both must take their direction from the gospel.

There will be a tendency for us to choose either authority or submission: to seek to be in control or to avoid responsibility. Neither option is acceptable. All of us are to practice mutual submission, and all of us are to exercise the authority of the gospel.

Think of the people with whom you live, work, and worship: family members; people in organizations and churches; employers and employees; and associates. Do you think of these people as over you or under you? What would be different if mutual submission were practiced by all these people, or if all authority were exercised as authority for others? That is what following Christ requires and what is expected of you.

Understanding Our Faith

7 Faith and Works

The "Son of Sam" serial killer had terrorized New York for months. Everyone was relieved upon his arrest. With all the media coverage, it came out that he had earlier gone forward and made a decision for Christ at a fast-growing church in Kentucky. On hearing of this, one woman responded on national TV, "At least he was a Christian." The statement was absurd, but it points to ideas of faith that are all too common within the church.

Why was the statement absurd? Isn't it true that we are saved by *grace* through *faith* and not according to our *works*? Could the "Son of Sam" killer have had faith despite his actions?

On the other hand, doesn't scripture constantly call us to obedience to God? And doesn't it consistently teach that judgment is according to works? What does God want of us—believing or doing? Is there tension between the two? How are we to understand the relation of faith and works?

The debate over faith and works is as old as the New Testament itself. Protestant Christianity has rightly focused on faith as the only requirement for salvation. Unfortunately, this has often implied that what a person does is of no significance. In effect people say, "Just believe; it doesn't matter what you do."

How did anyone ever conclude it does not matter what the followers of Jesus do? Unfortunately, this confusion is just one example of the many views of faith that do not do justice to the teaching of the New Testament. Such views leave us with a faith that will not accomplish our salvation. Such faith is the same as no faith at all.

This chapter seeks to treat the tension between faith and works by addressing three questions: (1) What does "faith" really mean? (2) Isn't it simplistic to think that faith alone is enough? and (3) Where do works fit in? We begin by setting aside misconceptions of faith.

Misconceptions of Faith

There are four major misconceptions of faith that should be rejected. New Testament faith is *not* a decision, a system of doctrine, the ability to believe the unbelievable, or a set of rules.

Faith is not a decision. Ask a person about his or her faith and you will usually hear about an experience that took place years ago. Evangelists have placed so much emphasis on the necessity of decision that people think that this is all faith is. Those who espouse a decision-oriented faith usually also have a corresponding emphasis on eternal security—the belief that if a person was once saved, he or she is always saved. But there is no security for this kind of faith. Simon Magus believed but so misconstrued God's purposes that Peter told him he had no share in the gospel (Acts 8:13, 21).

Salvation is not a transaction worked out with God at some point in time. Nor is faith some warm feeling we had in response to an emotional evening. Too many people find a false security in some act of the past. If faith is merely a decision on our part, then we have turned faith into a human work, something we do to accomplish our salvation. Decision is important and may mark the origin of faith, but it is not faith itself.

Faith is not a system of doctrine. Faith is more than an affair of the mind. It is not merely what we think. We are not Christians because we believe certain facts or theories to be true. Just as decision was important, so the facts and truths of the gospel are important. We cannot be Christians without believing that certain facts are true—notably the resurrection of Christ—but faith cannot be reduced to such doctrines. The comment in James 2:19 that the demons believe and tremble ought to make those with a merely rational faith very uncomfortable.

Faith is not an ability to believe the unbelievable. Faith is not, as one little boy put it, "believing what you know is not true." Faith is defined in Hebrews 11:1 as the conviction of things not seen. "Not seen" should not be confused with "impossibilities." When faith is understood as a quantity of believing, it borders on being understood as magic. Faith is again made into a human work.

Faith is not a set of rules. How we live is extremely important, but rules are not faith. To suggest they are is again to make faith a human work. It is common, in fact, for people to keep all the rules, appear "good," and still not have faith. The Pharisee in Jesus' parable of the

Pharisee and the tax collector kept all the right rules, but he did not experience God's forgiveness (Luke 18:9–14). A person can perform numerous religious acts and attend endless religious meetings and still not have faith. Just as faith is not what we *think*, neither is it what we *do*.

The root problem with these and other misconceptions is the assumption that faith is a part-time job. "Tell me what decision to make, what doctrines to believe, and what acts to perform so I can get it behind me and go on with life." But faith is not something that can be "gotten behind us." These misconceptions include a valid element of faith, but they are inadequate for salvation because they relate only to a piece of life.

Biblical faith demands all that we are. Theologians often teach that faith involves the intellect, the will, and the emotions. It encompasses all of our being. That is why Jesus warned would-be disciples to count the cost before they followed (Luke 14:25–33). It is also the reason the New Testament directs Christians to test themselves to see if they are in the faith (2 Cor. 13:5; 2 Peter 1:10). The concern of scripture is not for our feelings of security, but for the reality of our faith. The rich young ruler came to Jesus seeking security about eternal life. He went away distressed, for Jesus confronted him with the shallowness of his understanding (Matt. 19:16–22).

Faith as Relationship

But is it enough to say faith encompasses all of our being—our intellect, will, and emotions? Aren't we still inclined to think "Have I thought, done, and felt enough?" So far, our discussion of faith has focused too much on us. We must push beyond ourselves and see that faith is most of all a relationship with God.

When the Bible deals with faith, it describes God seeking his people and establishing a covenant relationship with them. This is true for both parts of our Bible, the Old and New Testaments. In fact, the word *testament* really means "covenant." God commits himself to a relationship with his people. He promises to be their God and to be faithful. People are asked to affirm their relationship with God and to be faithful to the covenant by the way they live. If we are to understand faith, we must see it as an expression of this covenant relation between God and his people.

Faith, therefore, is a *life lived in covenant with God*. It is the human response to the relationship that God has established.

In the Old Testament, God established a covenant with Israel and lived in the midst of his people. All of the focus on the tabernacle and the temple in the Old Testament is to mark the fact that God was present with his people. In the New Testament era, God established a new relationship that is open to all people on the basis of the life, death, and resurrection of Jesus Christ. The presence of God with his people is continued, but the focus is now placed on the Holy Spirit and on the individual in whom the Spirit lives. God is described as living with Christians both individually and collectively (see 1 Cor. 3:16; 6:19).

Usually when we think of a relationship with God, we use language of God or Christ living in us. We say that we have accepted Christ into our hearts. That language is correct as far as it goes, but it is a distortion of the biblical picture.

Paul, for example, rarely speaks of Christ in us (only

about five times, with the meaning of some of those passages debated). On the other hand, over one hundred times he refers to our being *in Christ*. The distinction is significant. With our usual picture, Christ is about two inches tall, and we usher him into some small corner of our hearts. We are still in control. To speak of ourselves as *in Christ*, however, reverses the image. Our whole being is in Christ, the Lord of the universe. As members of his body, we are made part of Christ (Eph. 5:30), and at the same time we are made part of other Christians as well (Eph. 4:25).

Authentic faith is *relational*. Christians are people who live in Christ, and reciprocally he lives in them. It is as if Christ were a sphere in which our lives are to be lived. He is the vine and we are the branches (John 15). To have faith is to live in and with Christ just as he lived in unity with the Father (John 17:21–22) and let that relationship direct his life (John 8:29).

But what does it mean to live "in Christ"? Mostly, it means that we are identified with Christ's death and resurrection. We are so united to him by faith that his death is our death and his life is our life. Faith, for Paul, involved both a dying with Christ and a rising to new life. The best definition of faith is found in Galatians 2:19–20: "I have been crucified with Christ. I am no longer living, but Christ lives in me. What I now live in the flesh I live by faith in the Son of God who loved me and gave himself for me."

In Philippians 3:7–10 we see Paul renounce all that had value for him so that he might gain Christ. His desire was to be found in Christ, know the power of his resurrection, and share in his sufferings. Paul describes this process as *being conformed to Christ's death*. The words may seem strange to us, but they are merely a variation of Jesus' own words about discipleship in Mark 8:34: "If anyone wishes to come after me, let that person deny self, take up his or her cross, and be following me." We find life by losing it.

Identification with the death of Christ means a break in our relationship to sin and to this world. A politician who was a Republican and then became a Democrat would not be welcome at a Republican rally. We should feel such discomfort when God is left out of the picture. Identification with the resurrection of Christ means *a transfer of lordship*. Christ is now Lord, rather than our own interests. As our politician who changed parties would be instructed by a new party platform, we, too, have realigned our lives and have a new agenda. This twofold identification with death and resurrection takes place at conversion and is witnessed to by baptism. But it is *not* just an act of the past. While it is past, it is also present and future. We are to live the death and resurrection of Christ daily. It is the pattern for our lives. We also anticipate the future when death and resurrection will be a reality for us.

Often in discussions of faith, people wonder, *How much faith is enough? How much is the human part and how much is the divine part?* To speak of faith as being in Christ or as identification with Christ obviates such questions. Faith can no longer be viewed as a quantity of believing. Faith is not what we are able to conjure up, but our living in the relationship that God has granted us with himself. We cannot separate our part from God's part, because our unity with Christ does not allow such separation. To say that a person has faith is not at all to speak of what that person does. Rather, it is to focus attention on the God in whom faith is placed. To say, "I have faith" is to say that God is a trustworthy God.

Is Faith Enough?

But isn't it too simplistic just to focus on faith? Isn't life more complex than that? Isn't it annoying to hear someone say, "Just have faith and everything will be all right"?

Life is complex, and faith is not magic so that we can escape dealing with struggles, suffering, and death. Faith understood as relation with God is not simplistic. It does not seek to get things with God finished; nor does it seek to escape the difficult questions of life. Rather, it faces all of life in the presence of God.

Still, there have always been attempts to say faith was too simplistic and that something else was needed. In fact, several New Testament epistles were written to reject the idea that something else is needed in addition to faith in Christ. In Galatians the problem was Jesus plus the law. In 1 Corinthians it was Jesus plus spiritual gifts, especially speaking in tongues. In Colossians it was Jesus plus spiritual experience (2:16–23). In each case Paul will allow nothing to be added to the gospel. All that is needed is faith understood as relation with God based on Christ's death and resurrection.

Church history has also witnessed various theories of a "second work of grace." The Puritans stressed faith and assurance of salvation. Pentecostals have argued for faith and a baptism of the Spirit. Wesleyans have stressed faith and entire sanctification. "Keswick" theology presented faith and the lordship of Christ. Sometimes the desire for "something else" was rooted in pride and the desire for something special for oneself. At other times the desire was rooted in a suspicion that others who claimed to have faith did not really know Christ.

The answer to all these attempts is the same as Paul

gave centuries ago. *Christ is all and all you need.* There is no second work of grace in the gospel. You cannot have Jesus as Savior without having him as Lord. You cannot be a Christian without the presence of the Spirit, for it is the Spirit that accomplishes conversion. There is no such thing as faith without sanctification.

Many of us know of two stages (or three or more) in the growth of our faith. That is part of what it means to grow in maturity. But such experiences cannot become the pattern for the proclamation of the gospel. The gospel offers us Christ and only Christ, but in him we find everything else. The text in Colossians 2:9–10 sums it up well: "In him all the fullness of the deity dwells bodily, and in him you have been made full."

Consequently, faith is enough, for faith is that which binds us to the Lord of the universe in whom are hidden the treasures of wisdom and knowledge. Faith has an *adhesive* quality. It attaches us to the Christ who is sufficient.

What About Works?

So what about works? What role do they play in our lives of faith? When Paul presented a gospel of faith apart from works, did he mean that works were unimportant, as some have maintained? When James said "faith without works is dead," did he mean that faith was not sufficient?

From the time of the New Testament itself there has been tension between faith and works. But when the terms are properly understood, the tension disappears. This time we are *not* caught between two truths!

The tension still exists for some Christians, though, because they perceive a contradiction between Paul's letters and the letter written by James. As we will see, there really is nothing contradictory in their teaching, since they deal with entirely different problems and use their language in entirely different ways. In the end, both of them reject perversions of the gospel.

In his letter, James's concern is about those whose faith has no effect in their lives. His purpose is to show the difference between a "dead" faith and an "alive" or true faith (2:17–18, 26). His conclusion is that any faith that is not an active faith resulting in acts of love is no faith at all. Dead faith is not valid faith. Paul would say the same thing.

If we ask, "Did Paul know of a faith that does not work?" the answer is a resounding "No!" In Paul's letters, the plural *works* often acts as a shorthand expression for the "works of the law" (for example, see Rom. 3:28; 4:2), which refers to human efforts to present oneself as righteous to God. In this context the word is almost wholly viewed as negative. On the other hand, when Paul used "work" in the *singular*, it is almost always a *positive* term that refers to the productive life of faith. It is this latter sense of the term that James is concerned with, and his conclusions are ones to which the apostle Paul would say "Amen."

Faith apart from a productive life would not be acceptable to Paul. In 1 Corinthians 13:2 he writes, "If I have all faith so as to move mountains, but do not have love, I am nothing." In Galatians 5:6 he writes, "In Christ Jesus circumcision accomplishes nothing nor does uncircumcision, but faith working through love does." The parallel passage in 1 Corinthians 7:19 is even more surprising: "Circumcision is nothing and uncircumcision is nothing, but keeping the commandments of God is." Such passages could be multiplied over and over, and the result would be the same. We are, as 1 Corinthians 15:58 puts it, always to be abounding in the work of the Lord.

There is no such thing as faith without obedience. In fact, Paul sometimes uses "faith" and "obedience" interchangeably (for example, in Rom. 10:16). Paul could even summarize his missionary purpose as seeking "the obedience of faith" among all the Gentiles (Rom. 1:5). When we consider the message of Jesus and the other New Testament writers, the result is the same. Everywhere there is the expectation that a life in relation with God involves loving obedience to God and love for our neighbors. There is no such thing as salvation without obedience. We cannot have faith without being faithful.

The only time there is tension between faith and works is when there is a misunderstanding of one or the other. There is no tension between faith and works because, properly understood, faith encompasses works and necessitates productive living. Faith *works,* but it does not use its activity to prove to God or people that the believer is righteous. My executive friend referred to earlier seeks to make corporate decisions in keeping with his faith. That does not make him presentable to God or better than other people. That is just what faith does. It has a new agenda and seeks to work it out. A life of obedience is not something separated from faith; it grows out of the relationship with God that we have by faith. Works are made possible by faith.

We need continually to hear the message of Paul. Works done on our own effort can never provide a foundation for life before God. That foundation can only be provided by God's grace. By faith we respond to

God's grace and are given the right relation to God that we could never establish on our own.

At the same time, modern Christianity has an even greater need to hear the message of James and the rest of the New Testament. Obedience and productive living are absolutely necessary aspects of faith. We have misunderstood Paul and ended up with a do-nothing religion. No wonder people ignore the church! We are like those in Titus 1:16 who profess to know God, but by their works deny him—people who are "detestable, disobedient, and unfit for any good deed." The words are harsh, but the biblical message is that one either lives the life or one does not have the life.

Understanding Our Faith

8 Grace and Law

What should I do? The young couple before me sought my blessing on their marriage. Both were divorced from previous spouses. The circumstances of her divorce had been straightforward enough, but his had been messy because he had been sexually involved with another woman. That was two years ago. Now both regretted the path they had taken and both had renewed their relationship with God. Which should be applied—grace or law? Grace would de-emphasize the past. Law would emphasize the previous marriages and not allow remarriage.

Todd, a pastor friend, came to me with a problem. People long unchurched were returning to his congregation, but they were not making any changes in their lifestyles. They still pursued the typical status symbols and thought nothing of "small sexual indiscretions." Should he offer grace to receive them back or should he insist on law so that changes occurred?

God's grace can be neither underestimated nor undervalued. Even though totally undeserved, by grace the death and resurrection of Christ have saved us from condemnation and destruction. By grace our identification with Christ brings us freedom and life with God. By grace we partake of the Lord's Supper and with astonishment sit in loving fellowship with the Judge of the universe.

We have received all things as a gift of God's grace. But there is another theme in scripture: God's law. Both testaments tell of the importance of keeping and fulfilling God's requirements for a holy life. How do we reconcile the gift of God's grace and the requirements of keeping God's law?

Nothing in our faith is more important than a proper understanding of grace and law. As Luther phrased it, "Virtually the whole of scriptures and the understanding of the whole of theology depends upon the true understanding of the law and the gospel."

The Starting Point

A discussion of tension within the Christian faith is essentially a discussion of the grace of God. Grace is the key in dealing with all our tensions—be it faith and works, pride and humility, strength and weakness, or whatever. It is what allows us to be human, to deal with our problems, and to progress beyond our failures. Grace is always the starting point in the Christian faith.

Even so, few words are repeated more and understood less than *grace*. If it has any meaning for the average churchgoer, grace refers to the free gift of salvation so that we can be saved apart from works. As important as this is, grace is much more than the entrance into the faith; it encompasses the whole Christian life.

The Greek word that we translate as "grace" *(charis)* was used to refer to "anything that causes people to rejoice." It carried the connotations of beauty, kindness, charm, favor, and even gratitude. Other words such as "joy" and "gift" are based on this same root.

In the Old Testament there are two Hebrew words used to express the idea of grace. *Ḥen* usually carries the connotation of favor. It expresses the attitude of a superior to an inferior and is most common in such a phrase as, "If I have found *favor* in your sight" (for example, see Ex. 33:13). Another word is *ḥesed,* which is usually translated "lovingkindness" or "faithful love." *Ḥesed* assumes the existence of a covenant, such as that between David and Jonathan (1 Sam. 20:14) or between God and Israel (Ex. 15:13). Together these two words present grace as the *undeserved, but unswerving, love of God.*

Grace is, first of all, God's unmerited acceptance of us. If faith points to the human response to God's covenant, grace points to God's action in establishing the covenant. But it would be wrong to think of grace as an attitude or as something separable from God. *Grace is not something God gives us, but God giving us himself.* Grace is God himself in his active goodwill toward humans. It is nothing less than the *power* of God at work for our benefit.

God is like a shepherd who goes out to look for the lost sheep or the father who runs out to meet the prodigal son. His shocking acceptance of us is modeled in Jesus' association with tax collectors and prostitutes. The message of all of the Bible is that God acts this way just because he is that kind of God. There is nothing in the people—be they prostitutes or Pharisees—that causes the choice. In Deuteronomy 7:7–9 the Israelites were told:

> The LORD did not set his affection on you and choose you because you were more numerous than other peoples, for you were the fewest of all peoples. But it was because the LORD loved you and kept the oath he swore to your forefathers that he brought you out with a mighty hand and redeemed you from the land of slavery. (NIV)

Grace is thus initiated by God and is an expression of his nature.

The ultimate revelation of God's grace, of course, is Jesus Christ. The incarnation of Christ is the ultimate expression of God's favor (2 Cor. 8:9). In Christ the grace of God has been *lavished* upon us (Eph. 1:7–8).

There are no limitations about who may receive it. We either take it as gift or we do not take it. As James Moffatt put it, "All is of grace and grace is for all." What we find in grace is a power that redeems life, establishes a relationship with God, and renders each person fit for service.

One of the amazing things about Jesus is the way he enabled people to tell the truth about themselves. That is what grace does. It allows us to face the truth. Paul found the acceptance that allowed him to confess his persecution of the church and still say, "By the grace of God I am what I am" (1 Cor. 15:10). This lesson came through for a friend who has had a hard life: a short stay in prison for armed robbery, a family that has failed, and a deficient educational record. For most people these facts would be an embarrassment, and while Tom is not proud of them either, jail is where he met Christ, and he has moved past his failures. Grace enabled him to start over, to go to school, and to relate effectively to people because of his experiences. Without apology, he can say, "By the grace of God, I am what I am."

Out of fear of being "exposed" we often hide the truth about ourselves. We do not want to risk being rejected. We want to be liked and accepted. Imagine Peter after Jesus' arrest. He slunk around the courtyard hoping to avoid recognition and physical harm. We act in similar fashion, hoping that our weaknesses and failures won't be noticed.

Grace gives us the freedom to pull off our masks. Think of John Wesley who was part of a spiritual movement while a student at Oxford. He met regularly with friends for Bible study and prayer and later was sent as a missionary to Indians in Georgia. The truth was that he was ill-prepared, and he failed. He wrote, "I went to America to convert the Indians; but, oh, who shall convert me?" What if Wesley had tried to fake it and appear spiritual? He would never have allowed Moravian Christians to lead him to faith, and the world would have been far poorer. God knew the truth about Wesley and knows it about us, too. He values us nonetheless. He woos us and desires to be in a relationship with us.

We would be making a big mistake, however, if we thought of grace merely as our initial acceptance by God. Grace is the starting point, is present at every point along the way, and is there in the end. To express it another way, grace is not just the threshold by which we enter into salvation; grace is the whole house. In Romans 5:2 Paul states that we have gained access by faith into this grace in which we now stand. Grace is the sphere in which we live. All of our lives as Christians is to be lived in the presence of an active, caring God. The same dynamic that effects our entrance into the faith is the dynamic by which we live.

It is no accident that Paul begins and ends every letter with reference to grace. In effect, Paul underscores that all of life is lived within the parameters of grace. When Paul encountered his thorn in the flesh, the message to him was that God's grace was sufficient (2 Cor. 12:9). The whole of Christian life is described as "under grace" (Rom. 6:14). Paul and Barnabas urged their converts to continue in the grace of God (Acts 13:43).

Grace is what we all need. If I could communicate anything to the seminary students I teach, it would be a sense of the grace of God. Some have a high estimation of their abilities and chafe others as they try to prove themselves. Others so lack confidence that they fear the work of ministry. Sometimes they feel both ways at the same time. Seminarians are not unique. We all know these feelings. But grace humbles and empowers us by revealing who really is in control. The act of God to accept us brings with it the power of God for life. Here is the foundation for living. We are enabled to stand because of God's gift. We are what we are by the grace of God. Grace, therefore, produces humility and confidence, provides release and challenge, and is both gift and demand. Grace is the essential ingredient that makes all else happen.

Cheap Grace

I know a pastor in Texas who went to visit an elderly woman in his small town. He had been at the church for a number of years and had never seen the woman at church. They talked for a while, and he shared with her the gospel. All the while she just smiled, but eventually she responded, "But pastor, I am a Christian. I walked the aisle when I was twelve. And although I haven't been to church for a number of years, I believe, 'once saved, always saved.'"

This is the danger of a superficial understanding of grace. People hear the message about grace and draw the wrong conclusion. On hearing that salvation is a gift and cannot be earned, people have said, "Fine, I'll take it; see you in heaven, God." People have made their "decisions" for Christ and have gone on living as if nothing had happened. Nothing has changed to suggest that Jesus Christ is Lord of life.

"Cheap grace" is the expression made famous by Dietrich Bonhoeffer in his book *The Cost of Discipleship*. Cheap grace is grace without cost, Christianity without discipleship, faith without following in the way of the cross. But the grace God shows us was costly for him because it cost him his Son. Grace received by us is always costly, for it will not leave us as we were. Grace comes as limitless forgiveness, but with it comes limitless demand. Surely Bonhoeffer learned that truth when he was put to death in a Nazi concentration camp.

If we are to avoid cheap grace, our acceptance of grace must be accompanied by obedience, gratitude, and the extension of grace to others.

Obedience. From Abraham to Paul, the message is the same: God's people are to be obedient. As strange as it sounds, they are to be perfect as their heavenly Father is perfect (see Gen. 17:1; Matt. 5:48; Eph. 5:1). Such statements are not intended to drive us to an awareness of our sins, nor are they intended to encourage perfectionism. They mean simply that we, as God's people, are to take our character from him. As Bonhoeffer sums it up, "Only he who believes is obedient, and only he who is obedient believes."

Gratitude. Our obedience, as all other Christian acts, has its foundation in gratitude. Thanksgiving is the foundational act of the Christian life. All else in the Christian life flows from true gratitude. In fact, the Greek word for "grace " is also used to express thanks. For example, although an English translation cannot show it, Paul's statement "Thanks be to God" in 2 Corinthians 2:14 uses the same Greek word *charis* that is usually translated as "grace." Thanksgiving is the response of a heart that recognizes and values what God has done. In the New Testament, religion is grace and ethics is gratitude.

The extension of grace. We are stewards of God's grace (1 Peter 4:10). Just as grace is the power of God at work *in* our lives, so it must be the power of God at work *through* our lives. Grace is not passive. If it has been received, it must be expressed. The same forgiveness and love God gives us is to be mirrored to others. Grace brings "largess" that keeps us from being small in our treatment of other people. In particular, the material possessions that we have as gifts from God are to be instruments of grace to the poor (Acts 4:33; 2 Cor. 9:8–9).

When grace has altered our lives, become the basis of our worship through thanksgiving, and is extended by us to other people, we will have avoided cheap grace.

The Enigma of the Law

But how are we to be obedient? What are we obedient to? How do we show our gratitude? What do we extend to others?

An answer to these questions cannot ignore God's law. No problem in understanding the Bible is more difficult than the law. How do grace and law fit together? One is gift and the other is requirement. We have seen that faith necessitates work and obedience, but do Christians have to follow the law?

Already in the New Testament there is evidence of numerous debates about the law (Acts 15; Titus 3:9). How does the revelation of God in the Old Testament become oppressive in the New? Christians sing, "Free from the law, O happy condition." But the psalmist sang, "Oh, how I love your law! I meditate on it all day long" (119:97).

Even in the Bible conflicting things are said about law. On the one hand, the law is a tyrant from which we are freed in Christ (Rom. 7:1–6), and it is described as a ministry of death (2 Cor. 3:7). On the other hand, the law is holy, good, and spiritual (Rom. 7:12–14) and was given to guide God's people in all they do (Deut. 6:1–8). Small wonder that there is little agreement in the church or among scholars on the subject of the law!

Virtually all of the negative statements about law in the Bible were written by Paul. Only Acts 15:10 and a couple of texts in Hebrews give negative statements from other New Testament writers. From the standpoint of his Jewish contemporaries, Jesus broke the law by his actions on the sabbath. He also changed how the law was perceived by what he said about clean and unclean foods (Mark 7:18–20) and by his treatment of divorce (Matt. 19:3–10). Still, the sabbath was important to Jesus (Luke 4:16; 13:16) and none of his recorded sayings ever suggests that the law was negative. On the contrary, he said that he came to fulfill the law, not destroy it (Matt. 5:17–20).

Paul's negative statements about the law stand in tension with his positive ones. In Galatians 5:13–14 he instructs Christians to fulfill the law through the love of their neighbor. A few verses later in 5:18, however, he states that they are not under the law. While in some texts it seems that the law is no longer valid (Gal. 3:24–25), in Romans 3:31 he argues that he does not invalidate the law, rather he establishes it. He even wrote that, "The law of the Spirit of life in Christ Jesus has freed me from the law of sin and death" (Rom. 8:2).

Because of Martin Luther and the Reformation, Protestant Christians have tended to emphasize Paul's negative statements about the law. As a result, law is often seen as the opposite of grace and as completely negative. The unfortunate consequence has been a downplaying of obedience.

To correct this imbalance we must listen to the whole counsel of scripture on this important subject.

First, law is an expression of grace. In some places the law is contrasted with grace in statements like, "You are not under law but under grace" (Rom. 6:14). However, there are many passages in the Bible where the law must be seen as an expression of grace. The Israelites in the Old Testament did not view the law as an oppressive burden. It was a gift of revelation from God that distinguished them from their idolatrous neighbors. In fact, the Hebrew word *torah* does not mean "law" so much as it means "instruction" or "direction."

Furthermore, the law did not come as legalism; rather it came as covenant. The ten commandments were given in the form of an ancient treaty establishing a covenant between God and his people. Keeping the commands did not establish that covenant. God established it by his grace. The commands told the Israelites how to live within the covenant. The law specified what their attitude and actions should be toward God and neighbor. The law was summarized rightly by Judaism and Jesus with two Old Testament texts: Deuteronomy 6:5, "You will love the LORD your God with all your heart and with all your soul and with all your strength"; and Leviticus 19:18, "You will love your neighbor as yourself." Paul and James likewise see the law fulfilled in the love command from Leviticus. All the detailed instructions in the Pentateuch are commentary on these two greatest commands.

Also, nowhere does the Bible present a way to salvation by keeping laws. The Israelites were called to be the people of God because of his grace. They were to keep his commands in obedience to the covenant granted to them. That obedience, however, was grounded in their trust in God and his pledge to them. Salvation always is by grace through faith, and such faith is expected to bring about obedience.

When the rich young ruler asked Jesus what he had to do to inherit eternal life, Jesus told him to keep the commandments (Matt. 19:16–30; Luke 10:25–28). Jesus was not suggesting that the young man could earn his salvation, nor was Jesus trying to make the man aware of his sins. When Jesus specified several of the ten commandments and the love command, he was trying to point to the intention of the law. The young man thought he had kept all these commands, until he was told to sell his possessions, give them to the poor, and to follow Jesus. Obviously he had not loved his neighbor as himself and was not willing to. Nor had he fulfilled the intent of the law by demonstrating allegiance to God rather than to himself. Jesus did not use Paul's language of grace and faith, but the understanding of trust in God and obedience to him is the same.

The whole Bible can be understood as an attempt to produce proper obedience to the law. Proper obedience excludes any legalistic observance. Rather, it seeks an obedience from the heart that knows that the law is summarized in mercy and in the love commands.

Despite all else Paul says, the commandments are still important for him, too, and one of his goals is that the commandments be fulfilled (Rom. 8:4; 1 Cor. 7:19). If law is contrasted with grace, it can only be law in some way other than God intended it. The law, as God intended it, was a gift of his grace. The law is a good thing, or in Paul's words, "The law is holy, and the commandment is holy and just and good" (Rom. 7:12). We neglect it to our peril.

The Negative Side

If the law is so good, how did it get such a bad reputation? The answer can only be that the law has been used for the wrong purpose. Any law can be subverted to something other than its original intention. As 1 Timothy 1:8 states, "The law is good if a person uses it lawfully."

The purpose of any law is to direct behavior. Thus, modern laws all have to do with actions. We would mock a law that tried to address our attitudes. Imagine a law that says we have to like the president! But biblical laws also often address attitude: "You shall have no other gods before me." "Honor your father and mother." "Love the Lord your God." "Love your neighbor." The commands regulating action, such as "You shall not make an idol," or, "You shall not steal," are intended to help the people understand how the attitude is to be put into practice.

The law has been misused because people have forgotten that it directs both attitude and actions. How does this happen?

Laws, to be of lasting value, must be codified, and either memorized orally or written down. This is a drawback. People inevitably come to focus on the statement rather than the intention. Legalism is the result. The prophets, Jesus, and Paul, all argued against substituting the letter of the law for its intention. (See Isa. 1:10–20; Mark 7:6–23; Rom. 2:28–29.)

Legalism can happen in two ways. People can do exactly what the law says and yet develop a scheme so that the intention of the law is nullified. The sabbath day's journey referred to in Acts 1:12 was the distance people were permitted to travel on the sabbath without breaking the law, about three-fourths of a mile. Some Jews found a way to go farther. They took food out three-fourths of a mile before the sabbath. Then on the sabbath they would go out and eat the food. Since they had established a new residence by eating, they could go out another three-fourths mile. Any time we do something to keep the law, but get around it, we violate it. The other avenue to legalism is to focus on the law rather than on God and our neighbor, the real concerns of the law.

The real problem with the law is not legalism, though. Jesus rejected the legalism of the Pharisees, but he never blamed the law. Paul, however, found that even the moral law, that part that he knew was good, brought death to him (Rom. 7:7–10). This negative role of the law is dealt with almost exclusively in Romans and

Galatians, letters dealing with the relation of Judaism and Christianity.

Paul viewed the law negatively because he saw it as *causing* sin. One purpose of the law was to prevent sin by giving us a knowledge of sin (Rom. 3:20). But something happens within us when the law points out what sin is. Suddenly there is an option that was not there before. If we are told, "Do not," there is something in us that says, "I will if I want to." The law incites rebellion. The temptation joined with our rebellion causes sin. This is Paul's point in Romans 7:7–10:

> I would not have known about coveting if the law had not said, "Do not covet." But sin, seizing the opportunity afforded by the commandment, produced in me every kind of covetous desire. For apart from law, sin is dead. I was alive once apart from law; but when the commandment came, sin sprang to life and I died. The very commandment which was supposed to bring life was found in my case to bring death.

But Paul goes on in the following verses to show that the law is not at fault. Rather, the law is a victim. The law was intended to curb sin (1 Tim. 1:8–11), but sin is enhanced by it. Sin has taken that which is good, the law, and used it for a negative purpose. Sin always attempts to turn the good into evil.

Because of sin, the law functions negatively in another way, too. Since the law brings the knowledge of sin, the law also exposes sin in our lives. The law shows how we have failed, and in doing so, functions like a prosecuting attorney. The law is negative partly because it brings charges against us that we cannot escape. This function of the law is necessary, but not very comforting.

The law is also negative when people seek to use it as a means of entry into relationship with God. This is what is at stake in the debate of the Jerusalem Council in Acts 15. Should Gentiles have to be circumcised and obey the law of Moses? Certain Jews in Galatia were trying to persuade the Gentiles to be circumcised. The answer of the Council, and repeated by Paul, is firm. A person does not come to God on the basis of his or her own efforts to keep the law. The law was not given as the ultimate answer; Christ was. The law was to help us and lead us to Christ (Gal. 3:24). By grace Abraham was given a promise, and he trusted God. That is and always has been the only way into a relationship with God. The message of the New Testament is that the fulfillment of that promise has taken place in Christ.

The law functions no better as a way of *maintaining* our relationship with God than it does as a means of entry. The means for both enterprises are the same: by grace through faith. When it comes to producing that which is right in our lives, the law cannot do the job. It can point in the right direction, but it has no power to accomplish what is right.

Finally, the law is negative because it leads to pride and boasting. If we rely on the law as the way to relation with God, we focus on our own efforts, rather than on God. The pharisaic attitude of prizing our own righteousness destroys our relation to God and to our neighbors. Such an attitude is sin.

The real issue with law is the company it keeps. If it is joined to sin, humanity apart from God, and death, it really is negative and becomes another tyrant enslaving us. If, however, as it was intended, the law is placed in the context of the covenant with God and the work of God's Spirit in us, then it is not a tyrant but a gift from God (see Rom. 8:2). The law is like a tool. It is just a question of whether it is in the hands of sin or the hands of God.

All of these negative functions of the law are contrary to what God intended with the law. We should not think, however, that Paul's statements were a cool rational discussion of the law. They were made in the heat of battle. For him, the gospel was at stake. What is wrong is not the law, but what his opponents were doing with the law. The law itself is good, and still has a role in the Christian life.

Living the Law

Many Christians think the law belongs to another era and is irrelevant for Christian living. This is heresy. In the light of Christ's coming we are to live the law by the power of God's Spirit. John Calvin referred to the "third use" of the law: In addition to giving knowledge of sin and curbing the unrighteous, the law is to profit the lives of Christians by revealing the will of God and by encouraging obedience.

We cannot, as some Christians, merely quote Romans 10:4—"Christ is the end of the law"—and conclude that is all there is to say on the matter. The passage is debated, but a better translation would be, "Christ is the *goal* of the law unto righteousness for everyone who believes." This fits much better with 3:31 where Paul claims he is establishing the law. Therefore, the law is not irrelevant for Christian living.

To say that the law is to be lived does not ignore the differences between life in the Old Testament and life after the resurrection. Many Old Testament commands are no longer in effect. The sacrificial system is not to be continued because the sacrifices were a shadow of the reality that came with Christ. Numerous laws, such as the dietary restrictions, are set aside as belonging only to the cultural framework of ancient Israel.

Many people distinguish between the ceremonial law (the sacrificial system, rules about cleanness, and so on), the civil law (guidelines for Israel's judges), and the moral law (such as the ten commandments). While these divisions are helpful, neither Judaism nor the New Testament makes them. Jesus did distinguish between God's intention for marriage as expressed in Genesis and the recognition of divorce in the civil law of Deuteronomy 24 (Matt. 19:4–9). He also distinguished between the less important and the more important matters of the law—justice, mercy, and *faith*—even though the lesser are not to be neglected (Matt. 23:23). We also need to remember that the elements of the law Paul rejected were those elements that separated Jews and Gentiles in his day—circumcision, observance of certain days, and dietary regulations.

The important fact is that a new covenant has begun with the cross, resurrection, and coming of the Spirit. While some concerns of the old covenant are no longer valid, the relationships with God and our neighbor are still the focus. What was wrong in the treatment of others does not suddenly become permissible. But now the Spirit is with us to empower us to live by the law in the new covenant.

The influence of the Old Testament law on the New Testament is obvious. Nine of the ten commandments are repeated in the New Testament. (The command to keep the sabbath is not.) Jesus said only those who do

the will of his Father will enter the kingdom of heaven
(Matt. 7:21), and the law is a revelation of the will of
God. Even faith is considered part of the law by Jesus
(Matt. 23:23). Particularly in John, Jesus directs his
followers to keep his commandments (14:21).

We have already seen that Paul, too, expected the
law to be fulfilled by Christian living (Rom. 8:4; Gal.
5:14). In addition, Paul encouraged the Galatians to
carry each others' burdens because in doing so they will
fulfill the law of Christ (6:2). Similarly, in Romans
13:8–10 the ten commandments and the love command
again receive emphasis. For Paul as well as the rest of the
New Testament writers, the law is to be lived.

Obviously, the concern with such a statement has
nothing to do with legalistic observance. We still must
discern how the law is to be lived in particular
circumstances. We also must distinguish between the
cultural expression of a law in the Bible and the
intention of the law, just as Paul did (1 Cor. 9:20–21).
There are numerous issues that the law does not treat
directly that we will have to address on the basis of the
law. But without question, the intent of the law is to
guide our lives.

In the end, there is no tension between grace and
law when both are properly understood. Grace comes as
free gift, but it brings responsibility. Law, too, comes as
gift that is to be lived out. Christianity has to have both
grace and law. They can only be opposed to each other
when one is misunderstood or misused. Law taken apart
from grace becomes an insensitive tyrant and is destructive. Grace taken apart from law becomes antinomian
and an excuse for sin (as Paul had to argue against in
Rom. 6:1).

There is an order to grace and law. Grace always

comes first. The gift of grace establishes us and calls us to act. Being precedes doing. Works, righteousness, legalism, and boasting in human activity have always been wrong and always will be. We cannot do the work of God until we belong to the family of God.

But do the work of God we must. No Christian may take God's grace and leave behind God's requirement. To belong to the kingdom is to be involved in the work of the kingdom. No Christian deserves the name who is not demonstrating Christ's presence in his or her life. No Christian institution—school, hospital, church, or business—deserves to exist except to the degree that it shows how changed lives do things differently.

Show me how a person treats family, associates, the poor, and especially those believed to be under him or her, and I will tell you of the quality of that person's faith. Tell me how institutions make decisions concerning people, and I will know whether they are Christian or not. Being Christian is not evidenced in what we say, the theology we develop, the books we read, or in the institutions that we build. The evidence of our faith is in the love of Christ expressed in our lives.

Understanding Our Faith

9 Freedom and Responsibility

Not too long ago my son did something I had asked him not to do—he got his ear pierced. As far as I was concerned, such an act made little sense and expressed all the wrong messages. When I stopped to think about it, though, what difference did it make? In itself it was neither a good act nor a bad act; it was a matter of choice and an exercise of freedom.

If you ask a non-Christian what his or her main complaint about Christianity is, chances are the response would be something like, "I don't like all the rules." "Christianity is just a list of dos and don'ts." "I don't like other people telling me what to do."

Unfortunately, these indictments are often true. Christianity gets reduced to a set of rules on par with, "Thou shall not pierce a man's ears." The church has too frequently been a barrier to freedom and a bastion of conservatism with regard to maintaining this world's structures.

Why are sermons on freedom so rare? Pastors preach "God and country" sermons on national freedom or freedom from sin, but rarely do they focus on the personal freedom that the gospel brings.

In contrast to this image of a legalistic church, our culture puts forth the ideal of individual freedom. We are free to do what we want, to vote for whom we want, to worship the God we want to worship, to choose the lifestyle we want to live, to say what we want to say. Like Frank Sinatra, we want to sing, "I did it my way." Nothing has a higher professed value in our society than freedom.

The principle of freedom is the substance behind our culture's emphasis on "rights"—from civil rights to women's rights. The rights movement has even been extended to cover such things as animal rights, abortion rights, and gay rights. All of these movements express our culture's ringing endorsement of freedom.

Yet we need to ask, What is *freedom*? Where does it come from and what is it for? Is anything wrong anymore?

We sometimes act as if the word *freedom* had been coined on the Mayflower. Freedom has always been a prized possession of humanity. The ancient Greeks wrote treatises on freedom, and it was a major concern for the writers of scripture.

The Bible's judgments on freedom do violence to many of our commonly held assumptions. Among other things, scripture reveals that those who strive to exercise their own freedom are actually slaves, that the church's "rules"—when understood correctly—are actually expressions of freedom, and that we will never find freedom until we are enslaved to our proper Lord.

A System of Tyrants

Everyone has to face certain limitations to freedom. We are limited by our bodies, our natural abilities, our histories, past choices, and too often by our sins. Many people in this world are dominated by oppressive government systems or poverty. Some—including those in "free" countries—are dominated and manipulated by employers, family, friends, societal structures, or by addictions to alcohol or drugs.

Furthermore, our freedom is compromised by every commitment that we make. Paul pointed out that people are slaves to whatever they give themselves to obey (Rom. 6:16; see also 2 Peter 2:19). We may commit ourselves to our jobs, to pleasure, to middle-class values, or to selfish desires, but then, by those things we are controlled. If we choose to drive a two-seater sports car, we can only take one passenger. If we choose to live in an environmentally sound way, we will spend time sorting and recycling used materials.

The issue is not whether we will be free, but which Lord we will serve. To think that we are free is only to be blind to the forces that manipulate us. Even as Christians who experience new birth in Christ, we are limited by the old age in which we live. Particularly, sin impinges on our freedom. As Jesus said, "Everyone who does sin is the slave of sin" (John 8:34). If the sin is egotism, we will do service to needs for recognition. If the sin is sexual titillation, we will find ourselves pulled toward people, magazines, or movies that meet our need, and we will be hampered in relating freely to people of the opposite sex.

Paul viewed our plight as being caught under a hierarchy of tyrants. The master tyrant is sin, for it establishes the other tyrants and brings judgment. In Paul's mind sin is not merely the individual acts we do, but a force that manipulates our lives. Hand in hand with sin is the tyranny of self. We can give ourselves over to our desires, but to do so is merely to give ourselves over to the tyranny of sin.

Serving under the tyranny of sin is tyrant number two—the law. Although God's laws perform a positive function by providing us with a knowledge of sin, they actually *increase* the possibility of sin. Sin twists the laws so that they are used in a way contrary to God's intention. We use God's laws as a means to justify ourselves by our own efforts. But since God's demands cannot be met by human activity, following laws cannot bring salvation, nor will it do as a way of life. Such attempts with the law are dehumanizing and a form of domination.

A third tyrant operating in close relation with sin and the law is death. Although the tyranny of death has been broken (see Heb. 2:14–15), it is still a reality that must be faced.

Scripture goes on to list many other tyrants that try to take away our freedom—from principalities and powers to our own inabilities or doubts. But the outcome for all of them is the same. Christ has overcome the tyrants.

The message of the gospel is that the master tyrant, sin, has been overthrown by God's action in Christ. By his grace God provides release from the punishment of sin (Rom. 3:24–26) and from the power of sin (Rom. 6:11–14). I do not mean to sound Pollyanna-ish, but there *is* release from sin. Gwynn, a former student, is for me a remarkable example of such release. He was so addicted to drugs that he began to act paranoid. He trusted no one and felt that people were out to get him. The police were, and he soon found himself in a Columbian jail for drug trafficking. In that jail he was led to Christ. He kicked his drug habit and has since become an outgoing and caring person who shares his faith easily. For him and for all of us, Christ has overcome sin, fulfilled the law, and conquered death and the powers. With Christ nothing can legitimately keep us from being what God intends us to be.

True Freedom

True freedom emerges from a "freedom of the soul"—a freedom from wrong desires, ignorance, and barriers within us that prohibit authentic living. We can never be free until we are free within. A friend recently confided to me that he had been sexually abused as a child and that formerly he had been guilty of abusing his own children. He could never know freedom without finding freedom within. Thank God he found release in Christ that enabled him to forgive, be forgiven, and piece his life together. That is the message of scripture. The Bible is a book about freedom, and the gospel is an emancipation proclamation.

For all its focus on law, the Old Testament is a message of freedom. The Exodus story is about God's liberation of his people. This story becomes the pattern by which God's redemption is described in the rest of the Bible. The year of Jubilee (Lev. 25)—when every fiftieth year debts were canceled, slaves were freed, land reverted to the original family owners, and fields were left unplanted—is a marvelous picture of freedom. With this recurring pattern of liberation no family was continually shackled by past failures and debts. The expected Day of the Lord is viewed throughout the Bible as a time when God will deliver his people from oppression.

What is true of the Old Testament is even truer of the New. The ministry of Jesus was a ministry of setting people free. The title of Ernst Käsemann's book expresses it well: *Jesus Means Freedom.* Jesus released people from the powers of the demonic, from sickness, and from the burdens imposed by legal traditions. He tore down the barriers that prevented women, Gentiles, and other "outcasts" from being accepted as whole persons. His offer of the kingdom invited all people to the banquet in his Father's house.

While other New Testament writers also speak of freedom, this message is most obvious in the writings of Paul, who is often called the "apostle of liberty." It was Paul's teaching on the freedom of Gentiles not to observe Jewish laws that led to his arrest. "For freedom Christ freed us" (Gal. 5:1) is Paul's summary of the gospel.

A glance at the theological words used for salvation shows how fitting such a summary is. All the salvation terms are freedom words. *Justification* means acquittal. *Redemption* refers to freedom or release that is obtained by the payment of a price (such as purchasing the freedom of a slave). *Reconciliation* expresses the end of hostilities. *Salvation* itself implies a rescue from danger.

Christian faith grants freedom because it involves a transfer of lordships. To live in Christ is to live in the sphere of his lordship. Only there may we have freedom. Only there are the various tyrannies broken. The ancient Greeks said that the key to freedom was "not caring." If Jesus is Lord, we will be free because we will not care for the wrong things. We will not care about propping up our egos or fulfilling wrongful desires. When we care for his concerns, we are free to be what we were created to be.

Responsible Freedom

So what does freedom in Christ look like? The biblical texts dealing with freedom sound paradoxical. They all contain words that seem to describe the opposite of freedom. "You were called to freedom, brothers, only not the freedom that leads to an occasion for the flesh; but through love *serve* one another" (Gal. 5:13; see also 1 Cor. 7:22). In 1 Peter 2:16 Christians are directed to live "as free, but not using freedom as a cloak of evil, but rather to live as *slaves* of God." James even wrote of the perfect *law* of liberty (1:25) which is fulfilled in loving one's neighbor as oneself (2:8). The fulfillment of freedom is love. The obedience that the law seeks is found in freedom, not in legalism.

Another "paradox" concerning freedom appears in the way Paul addresses the Galatian and the Colossian Christians. In both cases he argues against those who would lay down rules for Christian living. But then he proceeds to set down some "rules" of his own in the form of moral guidelines and ethical exhortations. For example, in Colossians 2:20–21 Paul warns that the Colossian Christians should not submit themselves to regulations such as, "Do not touch, taste or handle." But in 3:5–8 he instructs them to put to death and get rid of various kinds of sins. In 3:12–17 he gives directions for Christian living.

The key for understanding these paradoxes of Christian freedom is the recognition that we are not merely freed *from* the various would-be tyrants; we are freed *for* service to God. The most striking example of this is in Ephesians 4:28: "Let the thief steal no longer; rather let him work with his own hands that which is good so that he may have something to give to the person in need." The person who did wrong to satisfy his own desires is now working to satisfy the needs of someone else!

We are freed to love and live as God intends. When Paul prohibited certain kinds of activity and told his readers how they should live, he was not setting down his own form of legalism. He was describing what it means to live in Christ. A person cannot be guilty of sexual sins, greed, anger, and malice, and still live in Christ. Rather, a Christian must exhibit compassion, humility, patience, forgiveness, and especially love. To live in Christ is to be free. To be freed by Christ is to be freed to love.

Nowhere is the paradox of freedom and responsibility so clear as in 1 Corinthians 9:19–23, which is a statement of the principles by which Paul carried out his missionary activities.

> Although I am free from all persons, I have made myself slave to all that I might win as many as possible. To the Jews I became as a Jew that I might win Jews; to those under the law as under the law—although I myself am not under the law—that I might win those under the law. To those without the law I became as without the law—although I am not without the law of God; in fact, I am obedient to the law of Christ—that I might win those without the law. To the weak I became weak that I might win the weak. I have become all

things to all persons that I by all means might save some. I do all things for the sake of the gospel so that I might share in it.

Being wholly committed to serving Christ and his gospel, Paul was free to identify with the various groups that he served. In the end, it was this freedom to identify with others that led to Paul's arrest and eventual death. Dangerous, yes, but freedom is both the character of Christian living and the foundation for Christian mission. Christian rock music is such an example of identification and freedom. Christian thought is creatively expressed in a new medium to a different cultural audience.

Freedom Principles

Freedom is dangerous and easily abused, but it is nonetheless the fruit of the gospel. Still, the apostle Paul spent much of his time helping churches grapple with their new freedom in Christ. While the specific concerns may have changed in two thousand years, the underlying issues Paul addressed are just as relevant today.

Much of 1 Corinthians deals with questions directly related to the practice of freedom. The most obvious question is that dealt with in chapters 8–10: Should Christians be allowed to eat meat that had been sacrificed to idols (as most of the meat in the shops would have been)? While on the one hand, Paul forbade participation in idolatrous practices, on the other hand, he allowed freedom for people to buy and eat meat without worrying about whether it had been offered before as a sacrifice (since as mature Christians they knew that "an idol is nothing in this world and there is no God except the one God" [1 Cor. 8:4]). But if another person's conscience was offended, especially someone who was weaker in faith and tempted by idolatry, then Christians should abstain from eating meat.

From Paul's treatment of a similar issue in Romans 14:1–15:6, three principles are discernible that should govern our freedom.

First, each person should determine the validity of an action for him or herself. There are no popes, scholars, or friends who can pass sentence on an issue. "Let each person be fully convinced in his own mind" (Rom. 14:5). If we are to be judged for what we do, we should be fully assured in our own minds before we act. "The faith you have you should have to yourself before God. Blessed is the person who does not condemn himself by what he approves. But the person who doubts is condemned if he eats, because his eating is not from faith; and everything that does not come from faith is sin" (Rom. 14:22–23). Our freedom covers all things that are performed in faith and for Christ.

For example, genetic research has enabled people not only to choose the sex of a child, but to splice genes so as to limit possibilities of inherited disease. Is this practice an example of unethical tampering with life or responsible action that a person may choose? The validity of such action must be determined by the individual with full knowledge of the facts and in the full light of one's commitment to Christ.

Such an emphasis on the necessity of individual decision should not be confused with individualism. All our decisions take place in the context of a community (as the third principle will make clear). In the end, however, the individual is responsible for making mature decisions for the life that God has given.

Second, no one should reject other Christians who have different practices. "The person who eats must not reject the person who does not eat, and the person who does not eat must not judge the person who eats, for God has accepted him. . . . Why are you judging your brother? Or why do you reject your brother? For we will all stand before God's judgment seat" (Rom. 14:3, 10).

Christians do not have the right to judge fellow believers. The assumption underlying this principle is that the area of disagreement is a "nonessential" and that both persons are acting "for the Lord." If sin or error were the issue, the discipline of the church would be in order, or we would expect the kind of face-to-face confrontation reported in Galatians 2:11–14 when Paul objected to Peter's behavior. But when the issue is practice rather than principle, judgment belongs to the Lord. Nothing should be done that would break the relationship between Christians.

A friend of mine who is a single parent can spend significant time with his boys only on weekends. The boys are old enough to have opted out of going to church. My friend has temporarily decided not to go to church either, so that he can be with his boys. Some Christians will find his decision unacceptable even if he finds other avenues to fill the role of church. He made the choice in good faith and deserves not to be condemned or rejected.

Christians do not have to agree on such matters or on issues of taste, culture, or style. In fact, they are not expected to agree on such issues. The key ingredient for all Christians, however, is that their actions are done "in, to, and for the Lord." Given this motive and conformity

to Christ's character, differences in practice should never
be a basis for rejection.

*Third, we should deny our freedom rather than cause
offense.* "Make up your mind not to put any stumbling
block or obstacle in your brother's way. . . . If your
brother is distressed because of food, you are no longer
living in love. . . . For the kingdom of God is not a
matter of eating and drinking, but of righteousness and
peace and joy in the Holy Spirit. . . . Therefore, let us
seek after the things of peace and the things that lead to
mutual edification" (Rom. 14:13–19).

At first glance this seems to contradict our freedom.
Instead, it is the recognition that faith working through
love is actually the embodiment of our freedom. Freedom in Christ is *freedom for service* to others.

There are times when we will have to sacrifice our
freedom, but there are also times when we will have to
defend our own freedom or the freedom of others. We
are not at the mercy of the weaker parties. We are to
show concern and sensitivity to them so that they are not
offended or excluded from the community. Legalism is
never to be tolerated. The very fact that these people are
referred to as weaker persons implies that they should be
taught. The problem, of course, both in Paul's day and
in our own, is the identification of the weaker persons.
Our tendency is always to identify the weaker person as
the one with whom we disagree.

Paul concludes this discussion by calling us to
imitate Christ, who chose to edify and please others
rather than himself (Rom. 15:1–6). "Therefore, accept
each other, just as Christ accepted you, in order to bring
praise to God" (Rom. 15:7).

Most Christians today would grant that the Bible
does not require total abstinence from wine and other

alcoholic beverages. It does warn about the dangers and abuse of alcohol. There are still many people, however, who are offended by any use of alcohol. Christians who disagree over the use of alcohol should accept each other without any hint that the other folk are weaker or less spiritual. Also, in some situations, rather than cause offense, Christians may need to give up their freedom. The concern is the edification of the other person, not the exercise of freedom.

All three principles assume we are dealing with issues that are deemed "nonessential," those subjects that are not central to the faith. But determining which matters are essential and which are nonessential is itself an area where Christians disagree. Wars have been fought over what most would consider "nonessential." No doubt when Peter refrained from eating with Gentiles because Jews were present, he did not see himself as sacrificing the principle of the gospel. Paul thought an "essential" of the gospel was at stake and let Peter know it.

In defining that which is essential, we should put the emphasis where the New Testament does: on the character of God and the life, death, and resurrection of Jesus Christ. Such matters as the details of the second coming of Christ, ideas about what one eats or drinks, particular forms of dress, how and when we worship— all are nonessentials, as long as they are done "from faith" and "in, to, and for the Lord."

A crucial task for the church is to distinguish as clearly as possible between the gospel and that which is merely a cultural expression of the gospel. We tend to equate the way we look and act with what the gospel says we ought to be. However, there are numerous legitimate cultural expressions of the gospel, and none of them is necessarily more valuable than another.

A basic principle for discussions of freedom is expressed in 1 Timothy 4:4: "Everything God created is good, and nothing is to be rejected if it is received with thanksgiving" (NIV). Christians do not have to fear God's created world, but may enjoy it and use it wisely as we serve God.

Martin Luther summarized our paradoxical freedom this way: "A Christian is a perfectly free lord of all, subject to none. A Christian is a perfectly dutiful servant of all, subject to all."

10 Is God Active or Passive?

I was a carefree, newly graduated teenager. It was a nice summer day and I was cruising a Tennessee country road in my brother's red Austin Healey 3000. Then a blur and the squeal of brakes and I found myself involved in a near head-on collision. Fortunately, no one was seriously injured, but the car was totaled.

In a way I never had before, I began to question God's involvement in my life. Why didn't he prevent the accident? The questioning only increased when a few months later I received four registered letters stating that I was being sued for over a quarter of a million dollars. Didn't God care that people were not telling the truth about the accident? Did he cause the crash so that my faith could be challenged?

Such incidents and questions are among the most complex and difficult we face. Is God an active or a passive God? Does God "intervene" in our world, or does he take a "hands-off" policy so that we are left to ourselves? How much is God responsible for what happens? Does he act directly or only indirectly?

People usually hold one of two positions on this subject: Either they believe that God is in control and manipulates events to punish or bless people, or they believe that God created the world, wound it up like a clock, and has gone off somewhere to let it run on its own. The latter view was made popular in the nineteenth century and was called deism. Although not many Christians consciously hold to deism, many live their lives as if God is not really involved in our world. Clearly, deism cannot be squared with the Bible at all. But as it turns out the first view is equally deficient.

As long as life is going reasonably well, we can maintain our simplistic views of the universe. But when an event shatters our naïveté, we are left with nothing. For a colleague of mine, such an event was a fire in Chicago's Our Lady of the Angels School in which ninety-two children and nuns were killed. He wrestled over God's response—or lack of response—for years. How could God allow all those children to suffer and die? He no longer views life's occurrences as simply blessings or curses from God.

In 1755 there was an earthquake in Lisbon, Portugal, in which 60,000 people were killed. The theological aftershocks spread throughout Europe. Some, like Voltaire, gave up on religion entirely. Theologians had been describing this world as the best of all possible worlds, and suddenly there was nothing but death and destruction. How could God cause or allow such an event to take place and still be a loving God? Were the citizens of Lisbon more in need of judgment than, say, the citizens of Paris or London?

Reality is much more complex than we imagine. We

sometimes take only pieces of the Bible to placate our thinking. To try to understand God's activity in the world, we must deal with a host of related questions: Does God perform miracles? Does he have a plan for every individual and lead each person according to his divine will? Does he provide for people and protect them? How we answer these questions determines to a large extent how we live our lives.

Guided by Guidelines

People like certainty. But the Christian life is a life of *faith*—not sight. Humility and caution are required as we analyze what happens in our world. We cannot avoid interpreting events, but we must remember that our conclusions are based on *partial* understanding. If a tornado skips a church and destroys a bar, should we conclude that the tornado was sent as a judgment of God? What do we say if the tornado hits the church and misses the bar? That God wanted us to build a larger church?

The tensions in the Bible keep us from drawing what seem to be the "obvious" conclusions. At most, scripture provides "guidelines" for understanding God's actions. Hopefully, by following the five guidelines listed below we will be prevented from falling prey to a sometimes dangerous naïveté and become more discerning and caring about how God involves himself in our world.

First, humans cannot fully understand God and his actions. The biblical writers repeatedly describe the gulf between human understanding and God's actions. The prophet Isaiah bluntly states that God's ways and thoughts are not our ways and thoughts; in fact, God's ways are higher than ours as much as the heavens are higher than the earth (Isa. 55:8–9). The impossibility of explaining God's actions is shown in Job 38–42 when Yahweh ridicules the attempts of Job and his friends to explain Job's suffering. After wrestling with Israel's failure to believe in Christ, Paul concludes with words of praise marveling at how unsearchable are God's judgments and how his ways are beyond our comprehension (Rom. 11:33–36).

Second, God is present and active among his people. The deist position is wrong. God has not created the world and wound it up like a clock and left it to run on its own. The whole Old Testament testifies that God is active, that he calls, leads, and empowers his people. God is presented as Lord over the history of all peoples. Nations are presented as instruments by which God accomplishes his purpose, as when Assyria is used to punish Israel (Isa. 10:5–11) or when the Persian king, Cyrus, is raised to deliver them (Isa. 44:28–45:13).

In the New Testament the risen Christ promised, "I am with you always, even to the end of the world" (Matt. 28:20). The book of Acts emphasizes the activity of God's Spirit in the spreading of the gospel. Acts 17:27–28 also affirms that God is not far from any person, for in him we all live, move, and have our being.

Belief in an absent or inactive God will not do. If God is not in some way related to the events in our lives and has not acted to establish relations with us, there is no sense in speaking of him at all. To believe in God is to believe that he acts. The entire Bible is a record of the acts of God and an interpretation of those acts. Such events as the exodus, the incarnation, and the resurrection are the center of the biblical message. If God does not act, then the Bible is not to be believed.

Third, the God of the Bible is a hidden God. If God exists, why doesn't he go ahead and prove it to everybody? Yet Isaiah describes God as *hidden:* "Truly you are a God who hides himself, O God and Savior of Israel" (45:15 NIV). In Exodus 33:20 God tells Moses, "You cannot see my face, for no one may see me and live" (NIV). In John 6:46, Jesus explains that other than himself no one has seen the Father. These texts say more than that God is beyond our understanding. The point is that we do not have direct, physical access to God.

God rarely attempts to prove himself. He is present with us, but as an Old Testament scholar put it, God is an "elusive presence." He cannot be grasped and held by us. When we think we have him, he is gone. He does not respond in mechanical fashion to our rituals or our problems. He cannot be programmed and will not be manipulated. Neither he nor his actions fit into the boxes we create for him. When we act as if we know exactly what he is doing, we delude ourselves. As Pascal put it, "Every religion which does not declare that God is a hidden God is not true" (*Pensées,* 584).

Why does God remain hidden? No doubt, one reason is that God's holiness is too great for humans to endure. Another reason may be that for God to have authentic relations with people, there must be freedom; if God forces himself on us by overwhelming acts, then we are compelled into a relationship with him. Dostoyevski said, "Thou wouldst not enslave man by a miracle and didst crave faith given freely, not based on miracle." God does not coerce; he invites. To preserve human freedom he will even let people do the opposite of his desires and even let them abuse others. Because of human free will, God has chosen to veil his presence. He does not want automatons.

Fourth, God is not directly responsible for every event that occurs. Genesis 6:5–6 reports that because of human sin God was sorry that he had created humankind. God's grief shows us that much of what happens is not of God's doing. Job's friends attribute his suffering to God's punishment of sin, but Job, and later God, will have none of it. In Luke 13:1–5 Jesus likewise argues against a "straight line" interpretation of events, arguing that certain tragedies cannot be viewed as God's personal judgment on sin.

Saying that God is not directly responsible for every event does not remove the problem of evil. Even if God is not directly responsible, he at least allows suffering and evil to take place. But there is a big difference between God's permitting events and his causing them. If God causes evil, he must be held accountable for it. If he permits evil, the responsibility for it is placed on the free will of the persons doing it. We may question why God values free will so much, but there is no doubt that he does.

Being human means being responsible for our actions and being subject to the actions of others. Our neighbor has the free will to commit murder, and we could well be the victim of his free will. To be human means to be a resident of the old age where sin (ours and others'), suffering, tragedy, and death are all commonplace. God created the world, willing to chance what free human beings would do. God may be responsible for allowing such a world to exist, but he is not directly responsible for all the events that take place.

Finally, rather than doing things to people, God usually works in and through them and through the created order. In the Bible most of the activity of God is not performed directly by God, but through some agent. When he dried the sea at the exodus, he did so by a strong east wind (Ex. 14:21). In fact, many scholars interpret the first nine plagues on Egypt (Ex. 7–12) as a result of natural forces caused by extreme flooding of the Nile. In most all of the miracle narratives in the Bible God acts through nature, nations, and people. Even the healing miracles of Jesus usually engage the faith of the person. This is not an attempt to say how God must act, for he is free to act as he sees fit at any time. Nor is it an attempt to de-emphasize or explain away the miraculous. Certainly there are many events in scripture that do not take place through the created order, most notably, the resurrection of Jesus. We cannot put God in a box to control his activity, but we do need to recognize that he usually acts *through* creation rather than contrary to it. Acts within the created order are no less acts of God.

Does this mean we should or should not expect miracles? Despite what some in the church might say, this is not an easy question. Let me risk misunderstanding by saying that it is probably unfair to *expect* the miraculous. On the other hand—surely by now you will allow me the tension—we should be aware of the possibility of the miraculous and be *open to surprises* in the way God works. Clearly, however, God does not normally choose to suspend the creation order. There is an order to life, and still God is involved with us in his created order.

This interrelation of God and humans is far-reaching. We cannot separate God from the events of our lives. As Karl Barth stated, "The man [sic] who lives by his faith may know that in everything which may happen to him he has to do with God." What happens in a person's life may not have been caused by God, but God is involved. He shares in the joy or suffering. He provides, instructs, and calls us. The real issue is not so much who caused an event as it is how our relation with God shapes our response to events. No matter what happens, he is still Lord.

These five guidelines provide a framework for discussing questions affecting our daily lives.

Prosperity and Tragedy

Questions about God's role in our lives come into focus as we face issues of prosperity and tragedy.

Every religion attempts to help people escape the plight of the human condition: sin, fear, poverty, degradation, meaninglessness, future judgment. Some offer ways to bargain with God: "Do these sacrifices and you will be forgiven." "Wear this charm and you will be protected." "Keep these rules and all will be well." Or in a more modern framework, "Send ten dollars to support my TV program and God will bless you." It would be difficult to imagine a religion that did not offer the prospect of a better life for its adherents.

Christians are motivated by the same concerns as everyone else. People frequently turn to Christ because of fear and guilt and expect God to make their lives better and more meaningful. And there is nothing wrong with these motives or desires. The only difficulty in approaching God to make life better is the way we define "better," and how we expect it to be achieved. Do we expect God to change things so that we do not have to deal with the problems other people encounter? Do we expect some type of insurance policy that prevents tragedy? Are there things we can do or doctrines we can believe that insure prosperity?

The Bible sometimes seems to imply that prosperity

is the reward of believers and that tragedy is the judgment of God. Old Testament history tells how Israel prospers or languishes politically and economically directly in relation to whether she is obedient or disobedient to God. The writers of Deuteronomy and Proverbs repeatedly teach that obedience results in prosperity and that disobedience leads to poverty and judgment (see Deut. 28). Examples abound of persons blessed by God because of their faith: Abraham, Joseph, Daniel, and even Job both before and after his suffering. Examples of judgment on the disobedient are just as plentiful: the sons of Korah, Achan, Absalom, and Ahab and Jezebel.

Yet other parts of the Bible prevent our drawing any conclusions about prosperity necessarily being God's blessing or tragedy being God's judgment. The Bible is full of people who were prosperous though ungodly or cheats: Jacob, Laban, Zacchaeus, the rich fool, and the nations of Assyria and Babylon. While the Bible views wealth as a blessing in some contexts, wealth is seen in others as a burden making it difficult to enter the kingdom (Matt. 19:23–24). Still other texts denounce the rich (Amos 6; Luke 6:24; James 5:1–6). There are also numerous people who are righteous but poor, or the victims of tragedy: Job, Naboth, Lazarus, Mary, Paul, and even Jesus himself. The psalmists and the prophet Habakkuk often lament that the unrighteous are the ones getting ahead (Pss. 10, 74, 94), and the psalms frequently are prayers for rescue from distress.

Therefore, the Bible does not allow us to view prosperity simply as either a right of Christians or a reward from God. Neither does it allow us to view tragedy as simply something from which Christians are promised deliverance, or as a judgment of God.

When tragedy occurs, careful evaluation possibly will lead to some answers as to why the event happened, but we must also be prepared to live with unresolved questions. Two of my friends live with such unresolved questions. Their daughter was born with a breathing problem that kept her hospitalized for almost a year. She will be on a portable ventilator at least for another year. They had planned to be missionaries. Their daughter's health may make that an impossibility. Why did this have to happen?

At the same time, some tragedy may legitimately be seen as judgment. In fact, sin often brings its own judgment. A person who lives a violent life ought not be surprised to encounter a violent death. Selfishness and deceitfulness lead to very poor relationships. Sin is to be avoided, therefore, not only because it is wrong, but also because the punishment of sin is often sin itself.

Deuteronomy and Proverbs are right to connect obedience and prosperity. Wise and right living are necessary for a happy life, but they do not guarantee a happy life. We cannot say less than Deuteronomy and Proverbs, but we will need to say more.

When tragedy occurs, there may be numerous factors that are the cause. We may be the victim of someone else's sin, like a recent Chicago Christian who was murdered as she walked home, or like a child born with AIDS because of a mother's drug habits. Tragedy may result from ignorance as when a child climbs on high-voltage wires. It may result from negligence and malice as when a Korean pilot allowed an airliner to stray over Soviet airspace and was shot down. It may result from a whole society gone awry as with the Holocaust of the Jews. We live in a world where tragedy occurs for numerous reasons, and one where it sometimes is within our power—both as individuals and as a society—to prevent some tragedies.

In our fallen world, tragedy sometimes just happens—whether the victim is Christian or non-Christian, whether the person is living a holy life or a life of sin. The important thing for Christians in the midst of tragedy is not so much to be able to explain why it happened, but to determine what it means to live and hope in Christ in the presence of tragedy.

We should not forget that Paul and other New Testament writers viewed some suffering as *positive*. Suffering can be a means of identifying with Christ. It can also be a means of solidarity with the suffering of other people. The New Testament teaches that we cannot be followers of Christ without identifying with his suffering. None of us chooses suffering; on the contrary, we run from it. But Christians must know that there are borders beyond which we cannot run. Those borders are determined by the cross of Christ. Desmond Tutu, for example, could escape the horror of apartheid in South Africa, but his witness to God's truth and his solidarity with his people will not allow him to take the easy way out. The same borders are in place for all of us. We cannot relinquish the truth of God, nor can we turn our backs on people we are called to love.

The cross that Christians bear is the suffering they willingly endure in service to Christ. In Jesus' "farewell discourse" given just before his arrest and death on the cross, he promised his disciples *peace in the midst of pain* (John 14:27; 16:33). Christians can know peace in the midst of pain because they experience the presence of Christ in their lives and because they have a hope for the future. For this reason among others, the early Christians even rejoiced about their sufferings (Col. 1:24; 1 Peter 4:13).

In both our prosperity and our tragedy God is present with us, for in him we live and move and have our being.

Miracles and Healing

The place where Christians look most longingly for God's active involvement is in the area of health. When someone we love or even when we ourselves suffer, we long for God to work a miracle, to deliver us from our ailments.

Some Christians teach that God will perform miracles of healing if we only believe enough or if the right person prays for us. Some versions of this formula can be heard on several religious television shows. One preacher moves down a line of people; as he touches each person on the head, he says, "Take whatever you need. Take a miracle." Another says, "Send money as seed faith, and God will bless you." Still worse, another tells people not to go to doctors when they are ill, for all they need is faith in Christ.

The result of such teaching is often pain, grief, and guilt resulting from the fear that we are responsible for our suffering because we lack the faith to be cured.

The assumption that Christians ought never to be ill is simply wrong. Are Christians immune from the various causes of illness? Should righteous Christians never die? Do they merely live healthy lives up to the point of death? To be human is to be physically vulnerable to pain, injury, illness, aging, and death.

The statement that God does not want any of his people sick sounds valid. Of course, God would not choose sickness for his people, but the realities of evil and sickness are much more complex and involved than this kind of one-sided statement can allow. Sickness may have any number of causes: stress, aging, germs, sin, environmental factors, genetic factors, and who knows what else.

God can perform miracles. Many Christians, Luther and Calvin among them, have believed that miracles stopped occurring with the death of the apostles about A.D. 68. But God will not fit the boxes we create for him. He is free to work any way that he sees fit, but it is wrong for us to expect him to follow some mechanical formula or simply to wave some magic wand that solves all our problems. Faith is a significant factor in healing, but it is neither a guarantee nor a magic potion.

God is involved in the healing process as he is involved in all aspects of our lives. When we are ill, we should do exactly as James 5:14 instructs: Pray. Certainly we should take advantage of all the medical assistance available. God usually works through secondary means. Our suffering should be shared by the Christian community, and if we are restored to health, we should give thanks to God.

All of us, however, have to deal with the reality of death and the transitory character of life. If we are not restored to health, our only intention can be—like Paul's in Philippians 1:20–26—to glorify God both with our lives and with our death. We do not choose death; it comes as an unwanted visitor, resisted to the last moment. Still, we know that death is not the ultimate reality. Therefore, we can glorify God even in death.

What we have found in Christ is wholeness. The wholeness that we enjoy in this life, however, is partial, for the redemption of the body is still future (Rom.

8:23). Even while we are being continually renewed spiritually, our bodies are deteriorating (2 Cor. 4:16). By God's grace our bodies come equipped with an astounding healing ability. But they also come with aging mechanisms. That fact and the nature of the world in which we live insures that illness belongs to the human experience. There will always be circumstances of death and healing for which we have no explanation. But regardless of our circumstances, we are to enjoy the wholeness that Christ gives and to witness to that wholeness even in the midst of death.

Pointing the Way

Does God assist us and guide our lives? Without question, the teaching of the Bible is that he does.

But problems emerge when we look for God's activity in naïve ways. A boxer, after having just beaten his opponent senseless, exclaimed, "God helped me beat him up." A ball player trying to break a record said, "If the Man upstairs wants me to get the record, I'll get it." Catholics and Protestants in Northern Ireland pray that God will help them kill their enemies.

The problem is that we want God to provide for us what we think we need. We want him to bless what we are doing and to lead us where we want to go. But God is not our lackey. He does not do for us what he expects us to do for ourselves. He is not going to stop the universe for one of our whims.

When we speak about God's assistance or guidance, it ought to be in the context of giving our lives over to God's service. The leading and assistance we seek is to enable us to fulfill our role in his kingdom. We need his assistance and guidance to do his will. I do not mean that we need guidance merely in choosing a profession. More important, how shall our activities in life be opportunities for the kingdom? Whether a person is an insurance agent, a banker, or a clerk in a store, each needs wisdom from God about living effectively on behalf of the kingdom in that role.

When we seek God's will, we should realize that here, too, we live by faith, not certainty. People often claim that God has spoken when they have heard nothing but their own desires. We do not escape the effect of sin even when we are trying to serve God. When it comes to asserting what is the will of God, we need to exercise humility and caution. Even when we want God's will, it is possible for us to miss it. We may find the task of discerning God's will quite difficult. Usually, identifying the will of God is much easier in retrospect than in the process of trying to make decisions.

One of the most difficult choices I ever made was my decision to leave a teaching position in my own denomination to accept one at North Park Theological Seminary, which serves the Evangelical Covenant Church. My wife and I had no clear leading from God, but finally after a lot of prayer and pondering we made our choice. While there was some peace about the decision, for six or seven months there was no conviction of having made the right choice. Finding God's will is a process of discerning what he would have us do. Magic wands do not exist for finding God's will any more than for other areas of life.

We are correct when we seek God's provision for our needs and his leading and assistance for our lives. But we need to distinguish between our own selfishness and our dependence on God. All of our lives are to be lived in him, in accordance with his purposes, and on the basis of who he is. Only then is there meaning in our lives as God establishes the work of our hands (Ps. 90:17).

We all need to become a lot wiser and more mature in the way we think of God. God is both active and passive. God is passive when he allows our free will to be exercised, when he allows nature to run its course, or when he gives people over to their own choices (see Rom. 1:24–32). We can see that God is an active God when we view creation and other climactic events in the history of salvation, such as the exodus, incarnation, resurrection, and Pentecost. But God is active in other ways as he works in and through us and in and through the created order. God is active and often surprises us and moves in ways that we did not expect.

The very way we conceive of the question of how God involves himself in our world may be wrong. We separate God from ourselves and ask whether he is active or not. If we take seriously the truth of being *in Christ,* we ought not separate God from ourselves. The unity of God and his people is a reality. God is an active God in whom we live and move and have our being. He works in and through us to establish our lives and fulfill his purpose. The real question is whether we are active or passive in obeying God.

The ambiguities caused by the freedom of God, the freedom of humans, and the nature of this world results in tension for the way we respond. Both praise and protest are legitimate responses. While we are assured of God's goodness, we do not accept the legitimacy of evil. It is an invader into God's good creation. Prayer is the place where our tensions should be expressed most honestly. We may praise God's unsearchable ways with

Paul or protest with the psalmist and ask "Why?" when things go the opposite of the way we think they should. There is suffering that we choose in identification with Christ. There is another kind of suffering that we endure defiantly, knowing that it is part of this passing order. There is both reliance on God and active searching on our part. God is active and he is passive, and that tension requires a corresponding response in our lives. When people are victimized by evil like racism, even while they rely on God, they have a right to protest to him and other people. When people are hounded by a disease like cancer, even while owning death and God's peace, they have a right to protest defiantly the illegitimacy of sickness and death.

The ten-year-old son of some friends was killed in a bicycle accident. There is no way that I would tell them just to accept the fact of death, and certainly I would not tell them not to grieve. I grieve with them, even though we all look forward to the resurrection. My friends have a right to protest and to question. They also must know that God has identified with this suffering world in Christ and although at times seems distant, God is active in their lives and still brings peace to people in the midst of pain.

11 In the World But Not of It

A conference on life values for high school and college students included a mock auction. Each student was given seven hundred dollars with which to bid. Intellectual status was auctioned off for six hundred-fifty dollars. The value of working alone brought four hundred-fifty dollars. Profit and gain brought several bids for the full seven hundred dollars. Community had no takers at any price. We might say these students have accepted "this world's" values. But how could they help it? To be in this world is to be influenced by its value structure. Even when Christians do not realize it, "the world" impresses on us a system of values.

The imposing of this system of values has been so successful that the word *world* has itself changed in tone. When I was young, being called "worldly" was a negative statement. It meant that one probably engaged in sinful, hedonistic acts—activities such as dancing, smoking, drinking, and so on that Christians were taught to avoid. In fact, most enjoyable activities were looked upon suspiciously. Deep down, people feared that "if it is enjoyable, it must be bad."

Today being known as a "man or woman of the world" is desirable. It refers to someone who has been around and understands how the world operates. One credit card company used to have as its slogan, "Worldly and welcome." Pleasure has come out of the closet and is now the explicit goal and justification for many activities that used to be thought of as improper.

No one wants to be naïve, nor do we want to be suspicious of pleasure. But isn't the Bible rather negative about the world? How should we as Christians relate to the world?

When Christians try to understand their role in the world, one phrase quickly comes to mind: "Being in the world but not of it." This well-known but poorly understood expression is derived from John 17:11–16. Few concepts are more important for Christian living. No one can be considered a mature Christian who cannot give—and live—a legitimate explanation of this expression.

Different Worlds

Much confusion over how Christians are to relate to the world is due to a misunderstanding or at least vagueness in the meaning of the word *world*. The term has a variety of uses in the Bible. In fact, the expression "in the world but not of it" assumes two different uses of *world* in the two halves of the statement.

First, *world* can be a positive, or at least neutral, descriptive term. It can refer to all of creation or the universe (John 17:24; Rom. 1:20). Similarly, it may refer to the earth (John 6:14; 1 Tim. 6:7). Often it is used to refer to people, such as in John 3:16 ("God loved the world") or Romans 3:19 (". . . that all the world may be under indictment to God"). It can be used of the normal course of human activity, such as in 1 John 3:17 where "the life of the world" is used to refer to material possessions, or 1 Corinthians 7:29–31 where *world* refers to such activities as marriage, joy, sorrow, and business.

World can also take on a negative meaning. It can refer to the material world and all its "things," seen as objects unfit for human devotion when compared to life in relation to God (Mark 8:36; see also Col. 3:2). The strongest expressions of such thinking are found in James 4:4—"Adulterers! Do you not know that friendship with the world is enmity toward God? Whoever desires to be a friend of the world becomes an enemy of God"—and 1 John 2:15–17:

> Do not love the world nor the things in the world. If anyone loves the world, the love of the Father is not in him. Everything that is in the world, the desire of the flesh and the desire of the eyes and the pride of possessions, is not from the Father but from the world. And the world and its desire are passing away, but the one doing the will of God remains forever.

Both of these texts use *world* to describe the desire for pleasures and possessions that turn attention away from God. This meaning is very close to what Paul means by *flesh*. Both words refer to a merely human existence that takes no consideration of God. Love for the world obviously does not mean here what it does in John 3:16!

Several texts—especially in John—go one step further and include the connotation of hostility toward God and his people (John 15:18; 1 John 3:13). The world is seen as being under the rule of an evil power (John 12:31; Eph. 2:2) and a place of conflict (1 John 5:4).

It is important to be clear about what these negative uses of *world* are not saying. Two erroneous conclusions have been drawn from texts using *world* negatively. The first unacceptable conclusion is a negative view of humanity, which has caused some virtually to give up on the human race. The extremes of this attitude can often lead to a disdain and rejection of others as worthless. Yet it is the same biblical writers who make negative statements about the world who also speak of God loving the world, reconciling the world to himself, and sending his people to proclaim the good news to the world. Separation from God and hostility toward him do not cancel out the fact that humanity is created in God's image. He still loves and redeems such people.

The other unacceptable conclusion is that creation itself is bad. Since the elements of creation excite human desire to sin, some people have a negative view of the material world. The most common form of this error is to reject pleasure, especially sexual pleasure. A husband complained that his wife thought sexual intercourse was at best a necessary evil and sought to limit sexual relations as much as possible. That is an old story. In 1 Corinthians 7 Paul addresses some in Corinth who think that, even though married, they should not have sexual relations. Paul would not permit this attitude. The Bible does not reject sexual pleasure as evil; it rejects illicit sexual activity. Nor does the Bible suggest that pleasure or the material world is evil. On the contrary, the approach of the Bible is that "all God's creation is good" (1 Tim. 4:4). What is required of us is the right use of creation, not its rejection.

The number of meanings of *world* makes it difficult sometimes to understand what the word means in a particular passage. Occasionally, even in the same context, various meanings occur together. For example, in John 1:10 there are three different meanings of *world*. Jesus was in the world (became a human on this earth), the world (all creation) was made through him, but the world (people, specifically his fellow Jews) did not know him. As always the meaning of a particular word must be determined by its context. Nowhere is that more true than with the word *world*.

Dueling Sermons

In Jesus' prayer in the gospel of John, he states, "I will no longer be *in the world,* but they [his disciples] will still be *in the world*" (17:11). Almost any of the meanings of *world* could be understood in the phrase "in the world." We are in the universe, on the earth, and among people. We have lived a life apart from God or in hostility to God. But by paying close attention to the context, the last two options are clearly excluded. The disciples are to view themselves as in the world in the same way that Jesus was in the world. In other words, we live in the midst of human society.

The fact that we are in the world must be faced squarely. Too many Christians attempt to deny their humanity, but this little phrase "in the world" will not permit it. We have the same frailties, needs, and desires as everyone else. We live in this world with all its problems and pleasures. We share life with people of every sort, many of whom live as if God did not exist. Many are hostile to God. A philosophy professor announced on the first day of class, "In this seminar you cannot mention God in our discussions." On the other hand, many people rightly seek to fill the God-shaped void in their lives. We are in this world and any attempt to deny or diminish that presence is—if not sin—at least unrealistic.

We are in the world, but we are not of the world, or, another way of putting it, we "are not *from* the world" (John 17:14). In John 18:36 Jesus told Pilate that his kingdom was not from this world. He did not mean, as some people have thought, that his kingdom had nothing to do with this world. Rather, his kingdom did not have its *origin* in the world. His kingdom comes from God and therefore does not operate according to this world's scheme of things.

An appropriate paraphrase of "You are not of the world" might be, "The driving force behind your life is not this world, but God." Thus "being in the world but not of it" means being a human among humans, but not being determined by human life as if that is all there were. Christians are those whose lives are determined by Christ. This is what it means to say, "Jesus is Lord." He determines the goal and direction of our lives, and his death and resurrection are the patterns by which we live.

Christians have their true citizenship in heaven (Phil. 3:20). We are travelers and pilgrims (Heb. 11:13; 1 Peter 2:11–12). We are to think "the things above, not the things of the earth," for our lives have been hid with Christ in God (Col. 3:2–3). We no longer live, but Christ lives in us, and what we live we live by faith in him (Gal. 2:20).

The desires and temptations to be conformed to the

world around us cannot be denied. But they should not control us or determine who we are and what we do. The "world"—that human scheme of things of which we are a part—attempts to determine every aspect of our lives. Messages are sent in a thousand ways instructing us as to what is valuable and deserves our attention.

Several years ago a movie critic reviewed *The Hiding Place,* the movie about Corrie Ten Boom's experience as a Christian in a Nazi concentration camp, imprisoned for helping Jews. He had two complaints against the movie. He could not imagine anyone doing the things she had done, and he felt that the movie was preaching to him. Shockingly, he failed to realize that we get preached at all the time in movies, TV shows, books, magazines, newspapers, songs, or plays. What the movie reviewer was apparently reacting to was his discomfort with the message behind the preaching.

All mediums of communication offer some perspective of life, whether explicitly or implicitly. Often the message is blatant: "Sexual promiscuity is okay." "I am a material girl in a material world." "Greed is good; greed works." "Live for number one." At other times the message is more subtle, but it is there: A hotel boasts of its conveniences in an ad that reads, "Man [sic] does not live by room service alone." The specialists of this form of preaching are advertisers, whose goal is to manipulate us as efficiently as possible.

I am not suggesting that all the messages sent to us are bad or sinful. We cannot escape the attempt of the "world" to determine our lives. Apple growers want us to eat apples. Car manufacturers want us to drive their cars. If we close off one avenue of communication, there will be numerous others that we do not even recognize. Being in the world means being bombarded by messages about the way the world does things. Many of the messages may legitimately be viewed as positive. The orange detergent may really be better. Much will have to be faced squarely and rejected, for it will not fit into a life determined by Christ. When the message is that life is a game of sexual conquest, Christians cannot be duped into playing.

This is the crucial issue: What determines our way of life? Is it the world around us and our own desires or is it Christ? Whose sermon are we buying into: the Sermon on the Mount or the sermon on the "boob tube"?

There is another problem. Not only are we in the world, there is a sense in which the world is in us. We still live in the old age, and sin resides in our being. If "world" means a life apart from God, it points primarily to a life determined by human desires and pride. We are all guilty of that. Sometimes it is easy to see the message the world is sending from the outside without realizing the message the world is sending from inside us. We may separate from "the world" outside only to be determined by "the world" inside.

We feel this tension most acutely when it comes to material wealth. Christians claim to be citizens of heaven, but are often influenced more by the world's values in houses and cars than by Christ and his concern for the poor. One of my friends has a very attractive house and enjoys decorating it. When she tells me that she is a traveler and pilgrim passing through this world, I cannot help but tease her that she is really traveling in style. In such discussions the issues are complex. There is a tension between enjoying God's creation and caring for the poor and needy. However we resolve this tension, we must be careful that our choices are determined by our commitment to Christ rather than by the influence of the world around us.

Called to Be Separate

Some Christians resolve the issue of how we are to relate to the world by stressing the importance of being "separate." The phrase "separate from the world" does not occur in the Bible, but the theme of avoiding defilement is frequent. The classic text on this theme is 2 Corinthians 6:14–7:1:

> Do not be joined wrongly with unbelievers. For what do righteousness and lawlessness have in common? What fellowship does light have with darkness? What agreement does Christ have with Belial? Or what part does belief have with unbelief? What agreement is there between the temple of God and idols? For we are the temple of the living God, just as God said, "I will live with them and move about among them, and I will be their God and they will be my people. Therefore, come out from among them and be separate, says the Lord. Touch no unclean thing, and I will welcome you. I will be a father to you, and you will be sons and daughters to me, says the Lord Almighty." Since we have these promises, dear friends, let us cleanse ourselves from every defilement of the flesh and spirit, accomplishing holiness in the fear of God.

Separation is obviously important, but what is it? How far should Christians go in separating themselves from the world in which they live? The ancient community at Qumran, from which we received the Dead Sea Scrolls, went so far as to move out into the desert and establish an independent community. Monasteries and convents share the same ideal. In the past, some individuals became hermits for God, such as Simeon Stylites who lived for thirty years on top of a pillar.

Today Amish people are an example of Christians who take very seriously the Bible's call to be separate. They live apart, reject modern conveniences, and dress in "plain" clothes. The Quakers used "thee" and "thou" as a way to mark off their language from that of others. Some Christians refuse to vote or be involved in any non-Christian organization, because they think any involvement with secular systems will compromise their faith.

Some Christians practice separation for other reasons than to live holy lives. Unfortunately, many white Christians in the South formed private Christian schools rather than have their children attend racially integrated schools. In the North many Christians did the same thing by moving from the city to the suburbs. If a person fears those who are different or sees them as a threat to either security or purity, separation is a likely option.

Yet God's Word reveals to us that we cannot cut ourselves off from people and be righteous. We are to be travelers and pilgrims in this world, yes, but for the explicit purpose of being witnesses to those around us (1 Peter 2:11–12). How can we be witnesses if we are never with non-Christians? How can we be witnesses if we have cut ourselves off from the issues that society faces?

Jesus did not separate himself from sinful people. In fact, he seems to have been attracted to them. Prostitutes and tax collectors were part of his entourage. This was highly offensive to the religious people around Jesus. His willingness to associate and eat with sinners—the religious outcasts—was an important part of his ministry.

Being one of Jesus' disciples does not mean *less* involvement with other humans, but *more*.

No doubt many of us would have been uncomfortable with Jesus' association with sinners. The religious people of his day called him a glutton and wine drinker. And yet this is exactly the model we are to follow. Jesus' fellowship with sinners was a way of celebrating the coming of the kingdom (Matt. 11:19). These sinners found ready acceptance in Jesus' presence. In fact, he seems to have sought out the people who needed his presence most. And why not, if the good news really is a message of forgiveness?

We cannot escape our calling by saying, "Well, he was the Son of God; he could do it, but we cannot." Jesus must be the pattern of our ministries as well as our lives.

Paul's instructions to the Corinthians are helpful in this context. He had written in a letter, which we do not have, that they should not associate with sexually immoral people. But the Corinthians had misunderstood him. They thought he meant sexually immoral non-Christians. He had to explain to them that he was not prohibiting association with immoral people in the world, but with those who *claim to be Christians* and still live immoral lives:

> I wrote in my letter that you should not associate with sexually immoral people—not at all meaning the sexually immoral people of this

world or the greedy and swindlers, or idolaters. In that case you would have to leave this world. But now I write to you that you must not associate with anyone who calls himself a brother but is sexually immoral or greedy, an idolater or a slanderer, a drunkard or a swindler. With such a person do not even eat.

What business is it of mine to judge those outside the church? Are you not judging those inside? God will judge those outside. (1 Cor. 5:9–13)

We seem to have gotten things backward. We will tolerate a great deal from those who claim to be Christians, but are intolerant of non-Christians. We attempt to foist Christian values on a non-Christian world without providing the necessary Christian foundation for those values. We do have the responsibility to help society set its values and to point out wrong where it exists. But as Paul states in this passage, we have no business judging those outside the church. Our responsibility is to show the grace of God without condoning or ignoring sin. We are to call people from sin, not condemn them in it.

Separated to God

What will it mean then for us to be separate from the world? There are no easy answers here either. Individual decisions will have to be made in accordance with the purposes God has for each person.

We need to remember that being separate is first of all an act of God, rather than a human choice. Christians are people whom God has separated to himself. That is more important than being separated from the world. In being separated to God, we are called to live in relation to him. All of our lives are determined by this act of grace. Any choices that we make about the world must derive from our being separated *to* God.

The discussion of separation goes hand in hand with the discussion of the practice of freedom. Four principles are to guide our decisions on separation: (1) Christians separate themselves from sinful activity, not people; (2) Separation may be required to avoid misleading less mature persons; (3) Separation has to do with the focus of our lives; (4) We do not need to fear the world.

First, Christians separate themselves from sinful activity, not from people. Our first concern must always be to show the love and grace of Christ. We cannot do that if we are never with people. This is no excuse for engaging in sinful activity. We do not have to sacrifice principle in order to show grace. Contact with sinful people is not defiling. Only sin itself defiles. Paul was content to tolerate marriages in which Christian converts and non-Christian spouses lived together, as long as the non-Christian was content to stay in that marriage. Merely rejecting a business colleague who is unscrupulous gains nothing. I cannot condone or participate in his or her actions, but if I can accept and be friends with such a person, I have a chance to discuss the truths of the kingdom of God.

Sometimes relations with non-Christians include opposition or hostility to Christian commitment. Separation may be necessary in such cases. If so, people should know that the separation is not a rejection of them, but a rejection of the hostility to the gospel. In other cases involving hostility, separation may not be possible. Then the discussion must focus instead on a Christian's response to persecution. If a community rejects Christians because they take a stand against racism, those Christians cannot isolate themselves from the problem. They will have to band together and speak out against mistreatment of other races. Obviously, wisdom will still be the prime virtue in dealing with all such problems.

Second, separation may be required to avoid misleading less mature persons. When Paul discussed whether Christians could eat meat offered to idols (1 Cor. 8–10), he emphasized both Christian freedom and discretion. Where a practice may mislead a less mature person, it should be avoided. The well-being of people is more important than any action we choose.

Third, separation has to do with the focus of our lives. Typically, discussions about separation have been a debate about what acts or associations are permitted. Instead, more attention needs to be given to the focus of our lives. How do we spend our time? What nourishes our being? What are our true interests? What determines our lifestyles? To what extent do we live our lives as if God did not exist? By living in the awareness that we are separated *to* God, we will have taken healthier steps toward separation from the world than we would if all we did was simply follow a list of prohibited acts.

I do not mean to belittle the necessity of identifying specific acts that Christians should avoid. I am only concerned to avoid legalism and pharisaism. It is too easy to tailor our lists to our needs, condemn other people, and still not be separated from the world. If I reject abuse of alcohol, pornography, and sexual sin but am still guilty of materialism and preoccupation with status, I am still determined by the world. The Bible frequently lists sinful acts to be avoided, as in Colossians 3:5–9. Such lists need to be adapted with all seriousness. Christian conduct must conform to the character of Christ in decisions about our language, modesty, ego-centeredness, sexual relations, issues of justice, material wealth, and friendships. Relaxed standards in either individual or community ethics are unacceptable. Specifically, the cavalier and recreational approach to sexual relations will not fit in the Christian framework— no matter how hard people try.

Fourth, we do not need to fear the world. Christians are often paranoid, as if the world were a monster that is going to strip us of our faith. The New Testament shows that the early church was very much concerned about the world, but at the same time they were not afraid of the world. Paul knew that nothing could separate him from the love of God. In a real sense the early Christians viewed their mission as claiming back for God his lost world. The world is one of the things that Paul listed as belonging to Christians because they belong to Christ (1 Cor. 3:22). Because their lives were separated to God, the early Christians had confidence and boldness in facing the world and seeking to call it back into relation to God. The world may bring danger, but the person born from God conquers the world through faith (1 John 5:4–5).

Service to the World

I am not very good at remembering sermons, but a sermon from about twenty years ago has lodged itself in my mind. The text was an unlikely one, Colossians 1:2, which reads, ". . . to the holy and faithful brothers in Christ at Colosse. . . ." The preacher merely asked,

"What does it mean to Colosse [or wherever else we live] that we are in Christ and what does it mean to Christ that we are in Colosse?" The answer to these questions explains why we are in the world.

In Jesus' prayer in John 17, he said to the Father, "Just as you sent me into the world, I have also sent them into the world" (v. 18; see also 20:21). The disciples were given the responsibility of continuing Jesus' ministry. They were not left to hold on until the end, nor were they on some kind of retreat. Instead, they were given Christ's task of witnessing to the presence of God's kingdom and making that kingdom real in the midst of a sinful world. They were pilgrims and travelers, but they were not vagabonds. They had a purpose and a responsibility to the world. They were not of the world, but they were sent to it. That same responsibility and ministry belongs to every person who has faith in Christ.

Some wonder if this calling to serve the world means that Christians are supposed to change the world. Our answer must be, "Yes, but not the way some people try to change it."

Christianity would be a sorry religion if it did not change the world, but its task cannot be viewed merely in social or political terms. If we build housing and provide education, we accomplish much, but we have not provided real change in people's lives. The primary task of Christians is to witness to and make real the presence of the kingdom. The old debate between evangelism and the social gospel perverts both the evangelistic and the social concerns of the gospel. There can be no evangelism without social concerns. That would be like claiming to love without caring. Life in Christ will necessitate dealing with issues like poverty and injustice. As Sir Frederick Catherwood pointed out, "To try to improve society is not worldliness but love. To wash your hands of society is not love but worldliness." We are least worldly when we are showing God's love to the world.

An urban church nearby spends a lot of time helping people find housing or food or treatment for alcoholism. The needs are so great that they could easily become just a social agency to help people make it through another day. If they did, they would no longer be faithful to the gospel. But the invitation to worship and to hear the Christian message would fall on deaf ears were there not such social concern. It is the gospel that forces us to help.

Nor can there be social concern without spiritual transformation. Repentance and conversion are necessary in order to deal adequately with the problems the world faces. We do not merely ask people to be good. We ask that they be transformed by following Christ. But we cannot restrict love to those who choose to agree with us. The unconditional love that we have received is the love that we must show. Often that love must be demonstrated before we will ever be given a chance to be heard.

The relation of Christians to the world was discussed in a third-century work called the Epistle of Diognetus:

> For the distinction between Christians and other people is neither in country nor language nor customs. For they do not dwell in cities in some place of their own, nor do they use any strange variety of dialect, nor practice an extraordinary kind of life. This teaching of

theirs has not been discovered by the intellect or thought of busy people, nor are they the advocates of any human doctrine. . . . Yet while living in Greek and barbarian cities, according as each obtained his lot, and following the local customs, both in clothing and food and in the rest of life, they show forth the wonderful and confessedly strange character of the constitution of their own citizenship. They dwell in their own fatherlands, but as if sojourners in them; they share all things as citizens, and suffer all things as strangers. Every foreign country is their fatherland, and every fatherland is a foreign country. They marry as all people, they bear children, but they do not expose their offspring. They offer free hospitality, but guard their purity. Their lot is cast "in the flesh," but they do not live "after the flesh." They pass their time upon the earth, but they have their citizenship in heaven. They obey the appointed laws, and they surpass the laws in their own lives. They love all people and are persecuted by all people. They are unknown and they are condemned. They are put to death and they gain life. "They are poor and make many rich"; they lack all things and have all things in abundance. They are dishonored and are glorified in their dishonor, they are spoken evil of and are justified. They are abused and give blessing, they are insulted and render honor. When they do good they are buffeted as evildoers, when they are buffeted they rejoice as people who receive life. They are warred upon by the Jews as foreigners and are persecuted by the Greeks, and those who hate them cannot state the cause of their enmity. To put it shortly what the soul is in the body, that the Christians are in the world. (5–6)

Understanding
Our Faith

~~~~~~

12 Handling
Tension

During World War II, Winston Churchill was forced to make a painful choice. The British secret service had broken the Nazi code and informed Churchill that the Germans were going to bomb Coventry. He had two alternatives: (1) evacuate the citizens and save hundreds of lives at the expense of indicating to the Germans that the code was broken; or (2) take no action, which would kill hundreds but keep the information flowing and possibly save many more lives. Churchill had to choose and followed the second course.

Sometimes we, too, have to choose between two painful realities, but let us pray that God spares us from having to make too many of this kind. Often, however, we ought *not* choose between realities, for life is lived between truths that cannot be sacrificed. In such cases we must share both truths and live with tension.

Almost any issue in the Christian life could and should be dealt with from the standpoint of tension. As frustrating and unpleasant as tension often is, there is no escape from it. Tension is *always* present in our lives.

We live in a field of competing forces, each calling for our allegiance or attention. Jobs, families, churches, and our own needs lobby for our time. Individual recognition pulls against being part of the group. The demand for excellence clashes with the desire to be accepting and supportive. The inclination to show compassion argues with the fear about security. Judgment and mercy both want their say. Becoming a Christian diminishes the call of some of the old forces, but it also introduces new ones. We are given rest and called to work. We are asked to identify with the culture for the sake of mission, but to avoid being like the world. Most of all, however, becoming a Christian gives us a Lord who coordinates how we deal with these forces.

The major cause of tension is the nature of God himself. God is bigger than we are. None of our systems or doctrines can encompass God and his truth. Our attempts to reflect his concerns or his being are inadequate. When we have said all we know to say, there is always more that we cannot fathom. We may (and must) say true things about God, and what is important for our life with God has been made known to us. Still, God remains hidden and ungrasped by our best efforts. The mystery of God and his purposes is retained until the end.

Despite our desire for things to be simple, they are not. Christians always live in the midst of tension. We live *between* the truth. Because the gospel has placed us on firm footing, however, the tension is always peaceful and creative. The tension is peaceful because life has been given and the question of our allegiance has been settled. It is creative because it calls us to new life in Christ.

The Dangers of Tension

Real dangers confront us when we focus on tension. Not everyone will understand and we may lose friends. People may worry that they do not know where we really stand on some issues. One side may accuse us of giving ground to the "opposition," while the other side may say that we have retreated too far. When long-ignored biblical texts are allowed to challenge our neat theological packages, some will bring charges of "liberalism" no matter how unwavering one is in commitment to the scripture. For instance, Jesus' warning to fear him who can destroy both body and soul raises questions about belief in the immortality of the soul. Even to raise the issue causes alarm for some. But such risks are worth the price. Dealing with the tensions surrounding an issue is the only way to find the truth and keep ourselves from taking positions determined by other people rather than by honest investigation. But the way may be lonely.

A concern for tension may be viewed by some as a slackening of commitment or as a shaking of the foundations. For instance, rethinking male and female roles and relations has caused upheaval in the last two decades for our society. Christians are rereading scripture and finding suppressed teaching on mutual submission and on the equality of women. We cannot overlook any texts as we seek to redefine our understanding of God's purposes. But even when we feel the upheaval, dealing with such tensions is not a slackening of commitment or a shaking of the foundations. Tension does not give us two masters. We have only one—Jesus Christ.

A concern for tension is no more than the realization that the tile on which I stand at a given moment is not the whole floor. It is an awareness of the breadth and depth of the foundation which we find in Christ. Validity of our commitment to Christ or the correctness of our views is not evidenced in loud one-sided statements, but in wholeness, integrity, and obedience. Dealing with the tension involved in issues is evidence of real commitment to truth and a confidence that truth is not going to evaporate when all the facts are known. Truth is like a flower with deep roots. To enjoy it very long, we must take it all. If we take only the top part, it will wither in our hands.

Another danger in dealing with tension is that it can lead to copping out. People can become so overwhelmed by the complexity of issues that they give up on finding solutions. This is what is behind our culture's off-and-on interest in such issues as world hunger, pollution, long-running wars, and so on. The issues are compelling for a time, but the lack of quick solutions leaves us with feelings of despair and hopelessness. But biblical tensions should produce radically different results, because the ultimate coherence in our lives is provided by God's grace. We do not have to despair, because the Creator and Lord of the cosmos is sovereign and because the resolution of our conflicts is obtained from following Christ.

There is no value merely in pondering biblical tensions. They must be lived out. We are to resolve them in our daily lives. What does it mean to be free and responsible in my job and with my problems? How do both grace and law function in relation to the people around me? How should culture and gospel interact in our changing times? Each Christian must live out such tensions and determine how the gospel takes specific shape in his or her life.

The dangers with tension are real, but the dangers in dealing with only half of the truth are much greater. Tension cannot be ignored, for it will not go away. To focus on its dangers is as helpful as focusing on the dangers of breathing.

Holistic Thinking

Guidelines for living with particular tensions have been offered in connection with each of the topics with which we have dealt. But there are three guidelines resulting from our study on tension that deserve to be emphasized. Each is required for the life of the church.

The first guideline is to practice *holistic thinking*.

Holistic thinking is first of all humble. It recognizes our incompleteness and our liability to error. Humility is not always comforting when other people are looking for answers, but at least it is honest and does not mislead. Holistic thinking will not tolerate parochialism. Life viewed from one vantage point cannot do justice to the whole terrain. Conversations with other people from different perspectives will be required before firm conclusions are drawn. How could anyone dare form conclusions about male and female roles without listening sensitively to the concerns and problems of women?

No single statement can be identified with the whole truth. While a statement may be true as far as it goes, this does not permit it to be identified with truth. Every statement—even our most valued theological ones—requires qualification and explanation and is open to abuse. For example, in Galatians 3:28 Paul wrote, "There is neither Jew nor Greek, there is neither slave nor free, there is not male and female." This is a wonderful statement, but it requires explanation and must be paired with other statements. Paul does not obliterate distinctions between these groups; he obliterates *valuations* based on the distinctions. He was still proud of being Jewish and argued for maintaining distinctions between the sexes. He had no desire that women should become men.

Holistic thinking will cause us to look for tensions. When we know that a statement is true, we ought to ask what its limitations are, what other statements need to be made to prevent misunderstanding or extremism, and how circumstances might affect the implementation of the statement. We will have to become practiced in reading all of scripture to make sure we hear all of God's Word. We will also need to become practiced at reading people and situations in order to recognize tensions and apply the gospel to them. Tension is the framework on which the church does its work as well as its theology. We must both value tradition and seek new expressions of our faith. We must read texts that deal both with the certainty of salvation and the threat of apostasy.

Holistic thinking will also provide guidelines for the way we do biblical studies. With increasing frequency, critical scholars argue that tension within a writing is a sign of a later addition to the text. If Paul spoke of mutual submission in one text and authority in another, then the statement on authority is assumed to be a comment added by a Pauline disciple. Such a simplistic procedure cannot be accepted. Writers in the ancient world were not simplistic, and the situations they dealt with were as complex as ours. We ought to expect tension within a writer's thought both because of the nature of the material and the variety of situations that he had to treat. We do not understand any writer until we have dealt with all his writings and explained his apparent contradictions.

The results of holistic thinking will prove beneficial to the church. People will not find it necessary to separate their daily lives from their church life, because with holistic thinking, the problems and realities we would just as soon avoid are faced. Evangelism will be enhanced, for people will hear a message that is neither superficial nor unfairly biased. Resistance to change and change for the sake of change both will be lessened. People will neither cling to yesterday's answers nor throw out valuable tradition. Simplistic thinking will not suffice for our complex world. There are no easy answers, and the church should neither give them nor tolerate them.

Unity and Diversity

The second overall guideline for handling tension is to allow for *unity and diversity within the church*.

The variegated character of the Bible requires us to speak of its diversity. Its focus on God's relationship to his people evidences its unity. Paul used the metaphor of a human body with its diverse parts working together to describe the unity and diversity of the church.

Something embedded in human nature affirms both unity and diversity. Alfred N. Whitehead noted, "Men [sic] require of their neighbors something sufficiently akin to be understood, something sufficiently different to provoke attention, and something great enough to command admiration." This world would be an unpleasant place if everyone were alike or if no one were similar enough to others in order to relate to them.

Tension, with its recognition of the incompleteness of each person, requires both unity and diversity. Since we have partial knowledge and limited vision, we need the insight and perspective of other Christians to attain wholeness. Since I am married, single Christians will have to help me understand texts on celibacy. Christians who know suffering or loneliness can help others face these realities.

Our unity does not derive from the fact that we are from the same cultural, racial, or educational background, or the same economic level. Churches ought not be made up of such sameness, even though most are. Nor is unity something that we create. Unity is given from God and is based on our relation to Christ. If we are part of the body of Christ, we are members of him (Eph. 5:30) and members of each other (Eph. 4:25). To belong to Christ means that we belong to other people as well.

Our task is to maintain the unity that God has given us. This is accomplished by love and truth. Ephesians 4, which is a classic treatment of unity in the church, instructs us to put up with each other in love (v. 2) and to speak the truth in love (v. 15). At first glance, love and truth seem to be in conflict, but they go together. Love without truth is emotionalism. Truth without love is destructive. Together they preserve unity and lead to growth into Christ.

A very unrealistic student expressed his intention to serve as a missionary to Ireland. I was part of a committee that had to tell him he was being unrealistic in view of his gifts and efforts. The truth was gently but painfully conveyed. A few days later he came back to us and said, "Thanks for telling me the truth. I realize that I wanted to be a missionary only because my parents wanted me to be one." From that point on he could grow.

Unity is not uniformity, however, and diversity is just as important to the life of the church as unity. God seems to relish variety both in his creation and in his people. Grace is given to each person so that he or she may minister, and people are given to the church as gifts. People are equipped in a variety of ways for the ministries of the church. To focus on diversity recognizes the unique and necessary contribution of each person. Division is wrong, but diversity is essential.

The discussion of unity and diversity implies a parallel discussion of the tension between the individual and the community. Both are valued, and always there is a movement back and forth between the responsibility of the individual and his or her involvement in the community. In our day we have overemphasized the individual. P. T. Forsyth noted this tendency long ago and wrote: "Our peril, both in social politics and in religious belief, is self-sufficient and self-conscious individualism, ignorant of history and unequal to affairs. We have now too much individualism; what we have not is character." We say, "If it feels good, do it." We forget to ask, "What should I do?"

Individualism will not do. Despite the emphasis on the responsibility of the individual, Christianity focuses just as much on the community. Ours is a corporate religion. We worship and work together. We help each other understand the truth and do the many tasks of the kingdom.

On the other hand, the individual is never lost in the group, nor is the group to be blamed for the individual's action. In sects and false communities the group is always superior to the individual and controls the individual. Jim Jones and the Jonestown massacre are a painful demonstration of that. In true communities the identity of both individual and community is kept in focus. Each person has the responsibility to address and support others. If a person concludes that truth does not apply in his or her case, others in the community must bring the individual back to reality. If a person loses a job or struggles with doubt, the community must become a basis of support. The tensions in the Christian faith are an expression of both unity and diversity and of the importance of both the individual and the community.

Accepting Our Humanity

An issue that has repeatedly surfaced in our discussion of tension is the question "What does it mean to be human?" The gospel forces this question, for its purpose is to make us fully human.

Often people seek to avoid the limitations of their humanity. They deny the facts of their own existence. It is as if being human is not really good enough, but then, this attitude is as old as the story of the Garden of Eden. One definition of sin is the attempt to get out of life what God did not put into it. Sin is the refusal to be human. The attempt is understandable. Apart from a relationship with God, human existence does leave a lot to be desired. As valuable and wonderful a creation as a human is, there is no ultimate value or meaning for any person apart from a relationship with God. But then, God never intended his creation to be viewed separately from himself.

We must accept the limits of our humanity; when we do so, we discover that tension is inherent in our nature. Humans are made only a little lower than God (Ps. 8:5), but they are also like the beasts that perish (Ps. 49:12). Humans are temporal, but capable of unending relation to God. We are weak, but strong; have limited knowledge, but powerful and creative minds; are subjected to suffering, death, sin, and the actions of others, but are also capable of healing, and are free and responsible. Humans are victims of sin and temptation, but recipients of redemption and can live godly lives. Being human means that we have a variety of physical needs and drives: space, food, shelter, sex, and pleasure. It also means that we have less tangible, but no less real, needs and drives as well: recognition, meaning, productivity, relationships with other humans, and a relationship with God.

None of us can live authentically while attempting to deny these facts. Being human is not negative. There is a lot that is done by humans that is not Christian, but whatever is Christian is first of all human.

Denying our humanity or any part of it will only cause problems. As one person put it, "To live up to something one is not, one has to give up the little that one is—the condition of being human." In denying what we are, we lose the one thing of value we had— our humanity.

May God assist us to be as fully human as he intended us to be. To do so we will have to accept our impending death and anticipate the possibility of unending life with God. We will have to accept our limitations without denying our capabilities. Both the old age and the new will have to be dealt with. Our share in human suffering cannot be denied, but it can be reinterpreted as we suffer on behalf of Christ.

Living Biblically

To live biblically is to live wisely in the midst of tension. As Christians we live in both the old age and the new, and we are at the same time saint and sinner. We are part of a culture and in the world, but we are shaped by our relationship to Christ. We are at the same time inheritors, conveyors, and shapers of tradition. We are free from the law so that we may fulfill it. We have nothing in which to boast, but everything is ours in Christ. We identify both with the death and resurrection of Christ. We do not work for our salvation, but with salvation we cannot stop doing the work of Christ. In him we find the freedom to serve.

Tension allows us to live as whole persons and to do justice to all the gospel. Far from being frustrating or destructive, tension in Christ is truly peaceful and creative. Tension provides the joy of living.

In his little book *Balanced Christianity,* John Stott quoted a letter written in 1825 from Charles Simeon to a friend. The letter contained this imaginary conversation with the apostle Paul:

> The truth is not in the middle, and not in one extreme, but in both extremes.... Here are two ... extremes, Calvinism and Arminianism.... "How do you move in reference to these, Paul? In a golden mean?" "No." "To one extreme?" "No!" "How then?" "To both extremes; today I am a strong Calvinist; tomorrow a strong Arminian." "Well, well, Paul, I

see thou art beside thyself; go to Aristotle and learn the golden mean."

Simeon then commented on the imaginary conversation:

> But, my brother, I am unfortunate; I formerly read Aristotle, and liked him very much; I have since read Paul and caught somewhat of his strange notions, oscillating (not vacillating) from pole to pole. Sometimes I am a high Calvinist, at other times a low Arminian, so that if extremes will please you, I am your man; only remember, it is not one extreme that we are to go to, but both extremes.

Christians have the responsibility of holding both extremes and the middle in their hands and then of choosing how the tensions may be lived justly in each situation. The grace of God, which provides the coherence to our lives, is the power by which we live out our tensions. We live between truths.